The Strength Matters Training Series **1**

Maximum Aerobic Power

The ultimate performance program for everyday athletes over thirty who want to build a powerful aerobic engine and forge a heart of elastic steel

James Breese

STRENGTH MATTERS®

Maximum Aerobic Power

The ultimate performance program for everyday athletes over thirty who want to build a powerful aerobic engine and forge a heart of elastic steel

Strength Matters editor in chief: *James Breese*
Strength Matters editor: *Stephanie Panting*
Strength Matters guide editor: *Josh Kennedy*

Designed by *Strength Matters & aplusagency.eu*
Proofreading by *Strength Matters*
Typeset in *Gentona & Helvetica Neue Lt Std*

Made in Wales

Published by Strength Matters, Cardiff 2020
ISBN 978-1-9163103-0-8

Strength Matters, trademark of Strength Matters Ltd
www.strengthmatters.com

Dedicated to your inner athlete.

STRENGTH MATTERS®

MADE FOR **LIFE**

Introduction

Our Mission: To help people over thirty lose weight, get stronger, and live better.

At Strength Matters, we believe **there is a better way** for people over thirty to do health and fitness - a more intelligent, more sustainable, long-term approach that allows us to live life to the fullest means, well into our senior years.

We're obsessively passionate about fitness, and our mission is to help people over thirty achieve their maximum athletic potential without sacrificing their health.

We specialize in helping people over thirty live a fulfilling and athletic lifestyle. We believe that health and fitness for these everyday athletes is one of the least understood and least transparent aspects of the fitness industry.

We see that as an opportunity, and our gift to you.

We're excited to share our passion and simplify fitness for everyone over thirty through our education, resources, and community.

Life's better as an everyday athlete. Welcome to Strength Matters.

James Breese
Strength Matters Founder
Everyday Athlete

Table Of Contents

Life's better as an everyday athlete.

James Breese, Strength Matters Founder.

STRENGTH MATTERS®

MADE FOR **LIFE**

I am the Everyday Athlete

everyday athlete

/ˈɛvrɪdeɪ,ɛvrɪˈdeɪ /ˈaθliːt/

A person who prioritizes a healthy and physically active lifestyle in order to live life to the fullest.

In the U.S. and U.K., approximately 60% of all adults aged 18-64 are considered completely sedentary. They do no intended exercise, have completely inactive jobs, and spend more than 14 hours each day sitting on various types of chairs (couches, office chairs, car seats, etc.).

According to World Health Organization statistics, a further 20% of all adults do a little bit of daily movement but not enough to maintain health. Let's take a moment to reflect on this statistic. This means that 80% of the U.S. and U.K. adult population DO NOT do enough daily activity to maintain health.

80 PERCENT.

It's a statistic that astounds me every time I hear and see it. That leaves a remaining 20% of adults who regularly exercise to an adequate degree. But what does adequate mean?

This differs slightly from one government organization to another but, generally, it's considered 30 minutes of brisk walking or jogging per day and some regular resistance training to help with strength and bone density. I would strongly argue that this IS NOT adequate exercise and would question this from a professional standpoint, but it is a great place to start.

My personal and professional experience would guesstimate that less than 10% of the U.K. and U.S. adult population are doing adequate exercise to maintain optimal health, which is sad to me. Truly sad.

To me, that means that less than 10% of the adult population can physically enjoy everything life has to offer. Less than 10% of the adult population partakes in what they are able to do whenever, however they want. In my humble opinion, this needs to change. As a collective group of everyday athletes, we have a responsibility to encourage others to step up to join our humble society.

To grow the 10%.

Introducing the Everyday Athlete

An everyday athlete is someone who prioritizes a healthy and physically active lifestyle in order to live life to the fullest. Everyday athletes make the most of what they have, and they never settle for less than the life they are capable of living. It means being truly alive and awake - not asleep in some waiting room or on the couch.

Physical activity is part of the everyday athlete's DNA. It's not something they think that they MUST do, but rather a part of their day-to-day life. It makes them who they are. It defines them. As everyday athletes, we continually reach out for newer, richer, and deeper experiences. It's using those experiences as a means for personal growth and pushing our boundaries mentally, physically, and intellectually for the betterment of ourselves, our family, and the world at large.

Everyday athletes take an active role in our personal development. We are behind the wheel of our life, taking advantage of our unique and powerful potential as a person. We do things in life that motivate and inspire others to do something motivating and inspiring in theirs. We maximize our capacity to experience what life has to offer around us. This, in turn, expands our consciousness and results in an even broader range of life experiences.

The key to life as an everyday athlete is to open your mind and stretch beyond your comfort zone. If you're not being challenged or intentionally pushing yourself beyond the realm of things that are familiar, then the experiences you're having are no longer changing you. Anything that limits your ability to experience the breadth of life reduces your ability to live life to the fullest. If the point of living life is to maximize your capacity for taking advantage of what life has to offer, then this involves maximizing the length of your life as well.

> **"I don't want to get to the end of my life and find that I have just lived the length of it. I want to have lived the width of it as well."**
> **- Diane Ackerman, Author.**

Everyday athletes are not limited to the confines of a gym. They see the gym as a tool for maximizing life's experiences. They live for being outside the gym, just as much as they are inside it. Everyday athletes are not bound to any one tool, activity, or methodology. They believe in fundamental principles for health. From strength training to running, biking to skiing, team sports to individual events, everyday athletes embrace it all. They prepare for anything life could throw their way. They welcome the challenge.

Everyday athletes look beyond the hype and hyperbole of the fitness industry. They seek substance. They seek the truth. They seek clarity. Everyday athletes pursue performance but not at the sacrifice of longevity. Everyday athletes know they're in it for the long haul. Health comes first. No short cuts, no quick fixes. Everyday athletes work hard, knowing they will reap the rewards in the long run.

While living life to the fullest, everyday athletes collect experiences. They don't simply believe in knocking items off a bucket list. It isn't a competition to do

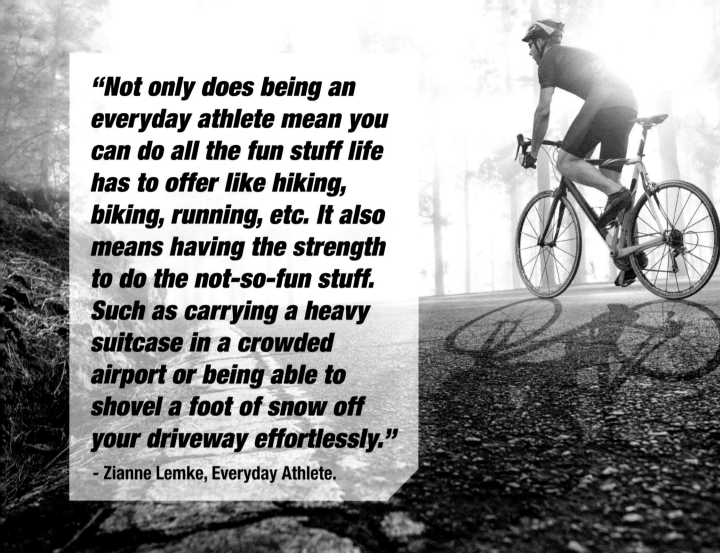

> **"Not only does being an everyday athlete mean you can do all the fun stuff life has to offer like hiking, biking, running, etc. It also means having the strength to do the not-so-fun stuff. Such as carrying a heavy suitcase in a crowded airport or being able to shovel a foot of snow off your driveway effortlessly."**
> - Zianne Lemke, Everyday Athlete.

the most things before death. For everyday athletes, it is about acquiring strength and wisdom from the challenges they overcome and having encounters that alter how they perceive the world. They draw from these experiences to lift others and help them raise their standards so they, too, can join the humble society of everyday athletes.

As an everyday athlete, you must make a habit of always reaching for new experiences that push you to grow and use your growth to have a positive influence on others. That is living life to the fullest, and that is the ethos that binds us together.

The Everyday Athlete Ethos

- I Love Life
- I'm a Work in Progress
- I Inspire Others
- I Embrace Challenge

I am the Everyday Athlete

Maximum Aerobic Power

The Maximum Aerobic Power Training Program is designed to help the intermediate and advanced everyday athlete build a powerful aerobic engine and forge a heart of elastic steel. This is a tried and true program that's been rigorously tested with our intermediate and advanced training clients who took their athleticism to the next level.

It will improve your strength levels and work capacity while simultaneously building your aerobic engine. We combine strength training and aerobic training without sacrificing any of your strength gains. By the end of the program, you will be in the best physical condition of your life, if you stick to the plan.

This program does not guarantee you success.

For that, you need grit, an iron will, and a lot of determination - but you also need to be strong and mobile. I can't emphasize this enough. You need a baseline level of strength and mobility before even attempting this program. Strength is a skill. Aerobic training is a skill. Combining both in a workable plan is an art form.

This book is about training your cardiovascular system to achieve Maximum Aerobic Power. You'll leave with a better understanding of the Strength Matters Hierarchy of Athletic Development, our unique training philosophy, and what it means to be an everyday athlete.

It comes in two parts: In Part One, you will discover our approach to cardiovascular training and learn about the different cardio training zones and how to develop them appropriately. In Part Two, you will

get the training program itself. The training program comes in three distinct phases. Do not skip a phase and do not go out of order. They have been designed as such to prevent injury and help you reach your maximum physical potential.

The Aerobic Power Zone is an incredibly important aspect of training the cardiovascular system. It bridges the gap between the aerobic and anaerobic thresholds, and is the gateway to anaerobic training performance. However, most people only ever live in the Aerobic Power Zone. They do not even realize other cardio training zones exist. Without developing the other zones, they are not training the cardiovascular system optimally. As a result, their cardiovascular performance is stunted and they never reach their true athletic potential.

Our goal with Maximum Aerobic Power is to help you break this mould and unleash your inner athlete.

Understand the theory, stick to the plan, **trust the process**, and I promise the results will follow.

I wish you the best of luck and all the enjoyment in the world.

Yours in health,

James Breese,
Strength Matters Founder
Everyday Athlete

This is the first time I've really felt part of a fitness tribe.

John Withinshaw, Everyday Athlete.

Train Anywhere. Achieve More.

We remove the shackles of working out in one location. Train any time with the equipment that's available to you. Your coach goes with you in your pocket and adapts accordingly, 24/7.

You'll be amazed at how much more you can achieve when working with a Strength Matters coach. Start your coaching journey today.

Visit **www.strengthmatters.com**.

STRENGTH MATTERS®

MADE FOR **LIFE**

Part One

Athleticism and the Strength Matters Hierarchy of Athletic Development

I was embarrassed. I was a trained professional but I couldn't run for three minutes at a relatively moderate intensity.

It was late September 2016. I was living in Melbourne, Australia, and it was the start of spring. The weather was turning and the days were getting longer. Little did I know at the time that this was the month that would change my whole life and business forever.

It was a Sunday morning, the sun was out, and my girlfriend at the time asked if I wanted to go for a run and then grab a coffee with her and her sister. I immediately said yes. I didn't think anything of it. Running was something I always USED to do. But this time around, I hadn't been for a run in a long time. In fact, a VERY long time. Six long years to be exact.

Running had always been a part of my life. Growing up in the mountains in Wales, playing soccer, rugby, and cricket, I didn't know anything else. But this time, I was 34 years old. I hadn't run for close to six years because I had gone deep into the traditional powerlifting, strength-only style workouts that my mentors, friends, peers, and colleagues were advocating.

"You need to keep getting stronger. Strength is the primary quality. Just focus on that," they said. And I did. I really enjoyed it too, at the time. Until I left the house for that run...

One of the Most Embarrassing Moments of My Life

We left the house and began to run. We headed down towards the beach. After the first minute, I could no longer hold a conversation with them. At minute two, I had to ask them to slow down so I could keep up. At minute three, I had to stop and walk. It was at that point that I looked at two people who I knew very well. They were staring at me, wondering what the hell was going on. It was the look that said, "James, you're a fitness professional. What is wrong with you?"

I was embarrassed. I was a trained professional but I couldn't run for three minutes at a relatively moderate intensity. I told them to continue on without me and I'd see them at the coffee shop. It took me close to 90 minutes to get there. By the time I reached them, they had already finished their coffees.

It was the most demoralizing, embarrassing workout I had ever done, and it was a big wake up call for me. It made me see my training from a completely different perspective, and with a fresh set of eyes I immediately added a walk/run protocol into my weekly workload. I was determined never to feel like that ever again.

Another Embarrassing Moment of Discovery

A few weeks later, around mid to late October, another chance conversation led me to consider a return to cricket—a dream of mine that had been dashed due to a shoulder injury. I had been running for a few weeks and was feeling good. I thought, why not? So, I went to the Tuesday night practice session, six years after I had last played, which coincidentally was also when I became serious about weight training and stopped running.

Looking back, I have no idea why I stopped playing cricket. It was such a big part of my life growing up. Thankfully, it is once again a big part of my life, but I know I'll never be able to get that time back. This will be one of my few regrets in life.

For those of you unfamiliar with cricket, there is a long-standing rivalry between England and Australia. So, a "Pom", as the Aussies like to call us Brits, turning up to play with them is kind of a big deal.

Once again, another moment of sheer embarrassment. It was like I had never played the game in my life. I couldn't hit or catch the ball, and my bowling was all over the place. Much to the Aussies delight, the fast bowlers kept bowling short at me, and the ball kept hitting me. I woke up the next day black and blue from the bruises. I hurt all over and felt like I had been run over by a bus.

Demoralized and with my ego shot to pieces, I wasn't deterred. In fact, it motivated me beyond belief, and I began to self-reflect and try to work out logically what was going on. Yes, I hadn't played for a number of years so I was rusty. But, similar to the running experience, it was more than that. Much more.

It came down to the simple fact that I was no longer athletic. I thought I was when I trained, but I wasn't.

I was strong but lacked any cardiovascular fitness. I was stiff and immobile. I wasn't agile, and my balance and coordination was all over the place. I was decidedly unathletic. I needed to become athletic again. I began to research everything I could about how to turn an aging athlete back into a lean, mean fighting machine.

What Is Athleticism?

With a professional head firmly on my shoulders - not an emotional one - I began to look at this question from a logical standpoint. I needed to stay objective. In order to become athletic, I needed to define athleticism and determine its key components and characteristics. It's an extremely objective word that means different things to different people.

Initially, I turned to Google, and here's what it came up with:

> **ath·let·i·cism, a noun.** the physical qualities that are characteristic of athletes, such as strength, fitness, and agility. "What he lacks in stature, he more than makes up for with speed and athleticism."

I'll be honest. This didn't really help much. There was I'll be honest. This didn't really help much. There was nothing tangible I could use, nothing specific I could take away. After weeks of searching for an answer, I realized that I had to take matters into my own hands. I presented to the Strength Matters team the seven components of complete athleticism, based on the original work of strength and conditioning expert Tudor Bompa. And so, it began—the hours, weeks, and months of endless debate and discussion. We finally agreed on athleticism as having ten key components:

The Ten Components of Complete Athleticism

1. **Strength** - the ability to create force

2. **Speed** - the ability to minimize the time cycle of a given movement

3. **Power** - the ability to create maximal force in minimal time

4. **Mental Resilience** - the ability to push yourself out of your comfort zone

5. **Aerobic Capacity** - the maximal amount of physiological work that an individual can do as measured by oxygen consumption

6. **Anaerobic Capacity** - the maximal work performed during maximum intensity, short-term physical effort

7. **Balance & Coordination** - the ability to perform movements with precision and grace

8. **Agility** - the ability to be nimble on your feet and move quickly from one movement pattern to another

9. **Stability** - the ability to prevent movement in one part of the body while creating movement in another, thus protecting vulnerable areas

10. **Mobility** - flexibility in motion, the range of motion through muscles and joints

Once we defined all ten components of athleticism, I thought we had put the entire debate to rest. I couldn't have been more wrong. We had a further six months of debate and analysis because of a number of questions that needed to be answered. Among them:

1. **Which component is the most important?**

2. **How do we assess each of the ten components?**

3. **What are the standards for each component?**

4. **How do we address the ten components in workouts and training plans?**

And that's how the Strength Matters Hierarchy of Athletic Development was created. It was designed to provide order, logic, and structure to the ten components of complete athleticism.

The Strength Matters Hierarchy of Athletic Development

After defining athleticism's ten key components, we set about prioritizing them in order of need. But this had a number of limitations. We couldn't order them from one to ten. It simply wouldn't work that way. We had to group them together because they are all equally important.

We looked at this process through the lens of building a house. A house needs solid foundations before you can build the structure and before you can apply the finishing touches. We created three layers of fitness - Layer 1, Layer 2, and Layer 3 - and grouped certain components together. We all agreed that we needed competency in key areas prior to others.

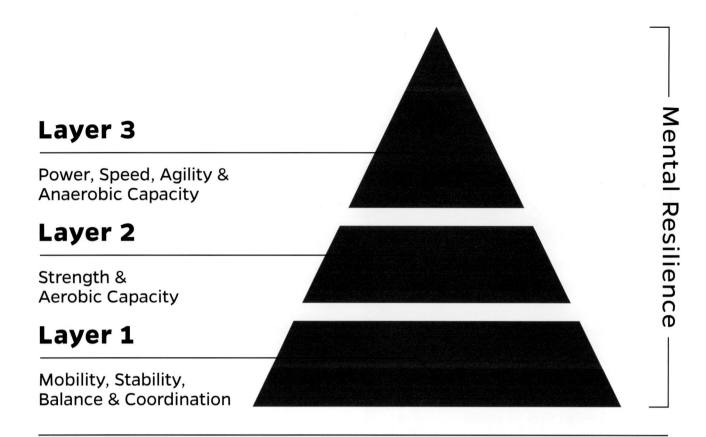

Layer 3

Power, Speed, Agility &
Anaerobic Capacity

Layer 2

Strength &
Aerobic Capacity

Layer 1

Mobility, Stability,
Balance & Coordination

Mental Resilience

FIGURE 1 - THE STRENGTH MATTERS HIERARCHY OF ATHLETIC DEVELOPMENT

Balanced Fitness and Athleticism

Our vision of balanced fitness and athleticism began to take shape, and the Hierarchy of Athletic Development was born.

As you can see, **Layer 1** is the foundation of the system. We need a base level of mobility, stability, balance, and coordination first. It's the foundation of the house. If we're deficient in these areas, we believe progress will be slow and the risk of injury heightened.

Layer 2 is strength and aerobic capacity. Once we have our Layer 1 base, we start to build onto it with basic strength and aerobic capacity work. This becomes the springboard to make the leap to Layer 3.

Layer 3 is the sexy layer, and it's advanced athlete territory. It's the layer everyone wants to jump to. It includes power, speed, agility, and anaerobic work (HIIT). It's also the layer that comes with the most risk. If you're deficient in any of the components of Layer

1 and Layer 2, it will show up here. This means that injury is more likely and peak athletic performance is hindered.

We decided collectively that mental resilience should be an overarching theme. It's important for all parts of life and athletic endeavors. Such was its importance, it needed this overarching theme. The Strength Matters Hierarchy of Athletic Development became a tool for us to identify areas of weakness that needed to be addressed, and morphed into a system that highlights the need to train our weaknesses.

It's a system that leaves nothing to chance. A system to help athletes reach maximum physical potential. A system to help everyday people reduce the risk and likelihood of injury. A system for people to know exactly what their weaknesses are and how they should train them. But more importantly, and selfishly, a system that would help this aging athlete over thirty reclaim his athletic lifestyle.

Hindsight Is a Wonderful Thing

I will always be thankful for that moment running in Melbourne. I will always be thankful for that day I went to cricket practice and got taken apart by the quick bowlers. They are probably the most pivotal points in my athletic career as an aging athlete.

Fast forward to today and I'm fitter, stronger, and more mobile than I ever was before. I'm back to feeling like an athlete again, but it wasn't an easy path. It's taken a lot of hard work, and trial and error. But it's given me hope. It's given me the ability to ski and snowboard, days and weeks in a row. It's given me the ability to play cricket again at a competitive standard.

Before that run in Melbourne, I thought I was physically athletic. I foolishly didn't consider that I possessed any weaknesses. I didn't consider the key components that comprised balanced fitness and athleticism. I thought being strong, and strength training alone, was the answer. The worrying thing was that I had ignored the warning signs. I had just carried on, as usual, thinking these things were normal when lifting heavy weights:

1. **I couldn't walk up a flight of stairs without getting out of breath.**

2. **My body fat % continued to increase and I didn't care.**

3. **Getting out of bed in the morning was becoming harder because I was more stiff and rigid.**

4. **I had to see a chiropractor or physical therapist regularly just to get rid of the pain.**

The list could go on, but these are the things that I think back on now. What was I doing? I personally focused only on Layer 3 work. For six years, I did power work and not much else. Speed, agility, and aerobic work were non-existent. Mobility, stability, and balance were an afterthought. And in terms of strength, I never went over 5 reps. Where was the muscular endurance and strength endurance work? I wasn't as elite as I thought I was. I came back to earth with a big thud. And I'm so glad I did, otherwise I think my forties, fifties, and sixties would have been very sad times for my aging body.

Applying the Hierarchy to Aerobic Power Training

We've defined athleticism as having ten key components and introduced you to the Strength Matters Hierarchy of Athletic Development. When it comes to our own athletic development, we need to remain objective and look at our fitness and athleticism through a clear, unbiased lens. We believe that this system allows us to remain objective at all times. It gives us a framework to make better decisions about what we need to address first. It's the framework that's applied to Maximum Aerobic Power.

Our system allows us to focus on our weaknesses. It prioritizes the body as one single organism, and emphasizes the fact that you're only as strong as your weakest link. We can assure you that training according to this system will lift your performance to dizzying new heights in all the activities you value the most. Failure to acknowledge your weakest components will lead to life-changing injuries and everlasting weakness. Heed my mistakes. Life as an everyday athlete with balanced athleticism is far more fun and enjoyable. Don't make the same mistakes I made.

Our system allows us to focus on our weaknesses. It prioritizes the body as one single organism and emphasizes the fact that you're only as strong as your weakest link.

What is Cardio?

I won't lie. It's hard. It's very hard. But the benefits for the body are endless and worth every moment you spend developing this energy system.

The Strength Matters Approach to Cardiovascular Training

The sad reality in fitness and the fitness industry, in general, is that two things sell and sell very well:

- **Sex, and**

- **Short, sharp, intense workouts.**

Over the past decade, maybe even longer, advertising and marketing companies around the world have been jumping on the HIIT (high-intensity interval training) bandwagon, proclaiming all you need for a good cardio workout is just 5 minutes.

Cardiovascular training is far more complex than throwing together a quick 5-minute workout designed to make you hot, sweaty, and sore the next day. In truth, there is no shortcut in cardio training. I won't lie. It's hard. It's very hard. But the benefits for the body are endless and worth every moment you spend developing this energy system.

It tries your patience, and you don't see instant results. This can be extremely hard for people to understand and apply because we live in a world of instant gratification. We expect instant results but the cardiovascular system doesn't work like that. It takes time. This is why people try to take shortcuts with short, sharp, high-intensity workouts.

Developing the cardiovascular system takes patience. It's about understanding the relationship of the aerobic and anaerobic energy systems and knowing where you currently sit on the cardio training spectrum. It's about understanding your own limitations and knowing what's right for you at any given time.

What Is Cardio Training?

Cardiovascular fitness is a good measure of the heart's ability to pump oxygen-rich blood to the muscles. We define cardiovascular exercise, or cardio, as exercising at a constant level of easy intensity for a specified duration, a minimum of 30 minutes, and potentially lasting hours in duration. It is performed at an intensity at which the cardiovascular system has the capability to replenish oxygen to working muscles. Cardiovascular training improves the ability of the heart, lungs, and blood vessels to deliver oxygen to the rest of the body.

There are two facets of cardiovascular fitness:

- **Aerobic** (with the presence of oxygen)
- **Anaerobic** (without the presence of oxygen)

Aerobic training, when done correctly, is sustainable and repeatable in nature. Typical activities include walking, jogging, cycling, swimming, jumping rope, stair climbing, and rowing. Anaerobic training, in a cardiovascular sense, when done correctly, is unsustainable and survival-based in nature. Typical activities could be short all out bursts in rowing, running, and swimming that last no more than four minutes. Aerobic training uses the aerobic energy system as its primary source of fuel, and anaerobic training will recruit the alactic and lactic energy systems.

Why Is Cardio Training So Important?

Cardio comes from the Greek word *kardia*, which means 'heart.' When you're doing cardio, it means you are exercising to improve the health of your heart.

The heart is, without a doubt, the most important muscle in the body. A healthy heart plays a vital role in human health. With regular and consistent cardio training for health, you can expect the following:

- **Lower rate of all-cause mortality**
- **Lower rate of cardiovascular disease**
- **Lower incidence of type 2 diabetes**
- **Lower rate of total body fat**
- **Lower rate of colon cancer**
- **Lower rate of breast cancer**
- **Lower rate of osteoporosis**

But cardio doesn't just play an important role in health. It plays a pivotal role in athletic performance. With consistent and well-thought out cardiovascular training plans for performance, you can expect the following:

- **Increased cardiac output**
- **Increased oxygen uptake**
- **Increased blood flow to active muscles**
- **Decreased sub-maximal respiratory rate**
- **Increased blood volume**
- **Improved thermoregulation**
- **Increased mitochondrial size and density**
- **Increased oxidative enzyme concentrations**
- **Increased capillarization in muscles**

If you want to reduce your risk of lifestyle-related diseases, make everyday tasks much easier with improved stamina and endurance, and reach your maximum physical potential, cardiovascular training is one of the most important aspects in your training.

What Constitutes Cardio Training?

It is a common misconception that anything that raises the heart rate is cardio. This couldn't be further from the truth. The heart adapts differently to weight training activities than it does to endurance training. During strength training, blood flow in the working muscles is restricted until the working muscles relax. This forces the heart to work anaerobically (without the presence of oxygen) followed by a rush of blood that enters the working muscles once they do relax. This means the heart has to works harder to pump more oxygen-filled blood to the working muscles, which causes an increase in heart rate but DOES NOT get more oxygen into those working muscles.

The heart must contract more forcefully to do this, causing blood pressure to increase and ultimately concentric hypertrophy of the heart (the heart growing inwards) to occur. This is not a desirable effect for a healthy heart. Strength training without a good cardiovascular plan can lead to a stiffer, less pliable heart. It makes the workload on the heart that much greater, blood pressure ultimately increases, and there is an increase in overall stress on the heart.

In stark contrast, endurance athletes who perform for long intervals have a consistent and regular supply of oxygen flowing to the working muscles. The heart grows both in thickness AND internal diameter. It remains stretchy and more pliable, which ultimately leads to an increased capacity to hold and pump blood around the body. This is eccentric hypertrophy of the heart, and is a very good thing.

Strength training and cardio training are two very different animals. We are not saying strength training is bad and you should stop immediately. Far from it. Remember, Strength does Matter! I'm just highlighting the fact that the heart needs to be trained differently based on your fitness goals, and the type of exercises you choose significantly affects how your cardiovascular system improves. That means you need to look at dynamic, low weight bearing exercises such as running, rowing and cycling as the go-to methods of cardiovascular development.

The more oxygen you supply to the working muscles with each contraction of the heart, the harder, faster, and longer you can perform.

How Do You Improve the Cardiovascular System?

When training the cardiovascular system, we want to:

1. **Increase the amount of blood pumped by the heart in one contraction**

2. **Increase the efficiency of the heart to deliver oxygen to the working muscles and remove carbon dioxide**

3. **Improve aerobic and anaerobic energy turnover**

In order to do this, we have to understand the three factors that determine cardiovascular endurance:

- VO2 Max
- Movement Economy
- Anaerobic Threshold

VO2 Max

VO2 Max is defined as the maximum volume of oxygen you are capable of taking up and using during intense exercise. It is measured in milliliters of oxygen used in a minute divided by the body weight in kilograms (ml/kg/min). It provides an aerobic power-to-weight ratio. As you now know, how the heart responds to different training methods, it is no surprise that those athletes with the highest reported VO2 Max in the world are cross-country skiers, runners, and cyclists.

In untrained men and women, their VO2 Max typically shows values in the range of 25-40 ml/kg/min. In elite athletes, these values will be between 80-95 ml/kg/min.

This is a considerable difference. The more oxygen you supply to the working muscles with each contraction of the heart, the harder, faster, and longer you can perform.

Movement Economy

How much energy does it cost you to move your body a certain distance? There are two elements to movement economy:

1. **Technical proficiency:** how well you perform the movement

2. **Metabolic economy:** the fuel source you use (fat or glucose)

With technical proficiency, you simply have to look at how a sub 2:30 marathon runner runs in comparison to someone who completes the race in over 5 hours. They glide through the marathon, while the latter struggles. They use less energy to cover the same distance with better technique, and go faster for longer before tiring. Metabolic economy is different. For sporting endeavors lasting more than sixty minutes, fuel stores become the major limiter.

There are two metabolic pathways that create fuel for the body: **aerobic metabolism** and **anaerobic glycolysis**.

Aerobic metabolism is the most efficient because it primarily uses fat as the fuel source, which is a virtually unlimited supply of energy. This takes place below the aerobic threshold (the point at which the levels of lactate in the body start to increase above homeostasis). Once you go above the aerobic threshold, you start to use a mixture of fat and glucose (sugar) as your primary fuel source. Once you go above the anaerobic threshold, it primarily becomes glucose. Glucose is not in plentiful supply, which can quickly lead to exhaustion.

When training the cardiovascular system, we have to think about the efficiency of the fuel source we are using just as much as how we improve the overall movement technique.

FIGURE 2 - Chart

Blood Lactate Concentration (y-axis, from 0 to 16)

Work Intensity (x-axis)

Low Intensity	Medium/High Intensity	High Intensity
	Aerobic Power Zone	
Aerobic Threshold		Anaerobic Threshold
Primarily Fat Metabolism	Mixed Fat & Sugar Metabolism	Primarily Sugar Metabolism

FIGURE 2 - LACTATE AS MEASURE OF INTENSITY

The Anaerobic Threshold

The anaerobic threshold is the maximum intensity at which lactate levels will remain elevated but stable for up to an hour. This is the point where lactate removal from the body cannot keep pace with the speed at which it is created.

Once above this threshold, every athlete knows you begin to slow down dramatically or even stop. Out of the three qualities, the anaerobic threshold is the easiest to train. However, as you will soon learn, to truly maximize your anaerobic threshold you first need to:

- **Have a great aerobic threshold**

- **Be strong enough**

The Strength Matters approach to cardiovascular training is underpinned by the concept that, *if you don't maximally develop your aerobic energy system first, and have sufficient levels of strength, you will never truly maximize your anaerobic threshold.*

How Often and How Long Should My Cardio Training Sessions Be?

This is one of the most common questions we get asked. It is also one of the hardest to answer because everyone's life situation is unique, as are their goals, willingness to train, and capability. So before we talk about how long and how often you should be training the cardiovascular system, we need to establish some ground rules:

1. A cardiovascular training session can be either aerobic or anaerobic in nature. It depends on the ability of the individual and what they are training for.

2. An aerobic training session will be a minimum of 30 minutes of steady state continuous activity which is easy and repeatable in nature.

3. An anaerobic training session will consist of a number of intervals and could last anywhere from 10-60 minutes depending on the athlete.

4. If done correctly, training aerobically can be done anywhere from four to seven times a week.

5. Anaerobic training needs a minimum rest of 48 hours between training sessions.

6. Aerobic training makes up 80-90% of the annual work load.

7. Anaerobic makes up 10 - 20% of the annual work load.

8. Before you can partake in anaerobic training, you need to be strong enough and have a robust aerobic system.

9. HIIT is the last thing we employ when trying to build a robust cardiovascular engine.

As you can see, there are many moving parts to create the perfect cardio training plan. It's not quite as simple as saying, "Just do three hours a week and you'll be fine."

Building the cardiovascular system takes time. You can't rush it. The human body is still the human body, no matter how advanced we get with technology. It still takes 9 months to have a baby.

Cardiovascular Training and Maximum Aerobic Power Training

Developing the cardiovascular system takes time and patience. It's about understanding the relationship of the aerobic and anaerobic energy systems and knowing where you currently are on the cardio training spectrum.

Volume, consistency, and patience are key to cardiovascular success, combined with the working knowledge of the importance of strength training and the development of the aerobic energy system prior to working the anaerobic energy system.

Strength training develops the heart differently to traditional cardiovascular training. Strength training actually restricts blood to the working muscles and encourages the concentric development of the heart, resulting in greater heart stress, whereas cardiovascular training encourages a continuous supply of blood throughout the body and develops the heart eccentrically.

Remember our model of cardiovascular development:

If you don't maximally develop your aerobic energy system first and have sufficient levels of strength, you will never truly maximize your anaerobic threshold.

Let's take Kilian Jornet, one of the greatest ultra-trail runners ever. His annual training volume is over 1,250 hours a year, or an average of 24 hours a week. Consider elite marathon runner Eliud Kipchoge, who is the first person to break the two hour marathon record. He averages 120 miles of running a week. The average club runner is lucky to average 40 miles per week. Building a robust cardiovascular system takes dedication and commitment. You cannot build it with a few ten-minute HIIT sessions a week.

If you're a true beginner, 100% of your weekly training time will be aerobic in nature. That means NO HIIT workouts. Remember, aerobic threshold development and strength training come first.

"Life begins at the end of your comfort zone."

Neale Donald Walsh, Author.

STRENGTH
MATTERS®

MADE FOR **LIFE**

What is the Aerobic Threshold?

Aerobic threshold corresponds to the most important training zone to use in developing aerobic capacity.

The aerobic threshold is the uppermost limit of exercise when the production of energy starts to become dominated by anaerobic glycolysis (sugars) rather than the oxidation (aerobic in nature) of fats.

It is an important marker of intensity for endurance athletes. It corresponds to the most important training zone to use in developing aerobic capacity. Without first maximizing your aerobic threshold or base levels of strength, you will never truly maximize your anaerobic threshold or VO2 Max, the gold standard indicators in measuring one's potential cardiovascular performance. In scientific terms, the aerobic threshold is at the point that blood lactate begins to rise above the normal resting level of 2mmol/L (millimole per litre).

It's important to understand the role of lactic acid, which is often seen as the cause of poor cardiovascular capacity. Lactic acid only appears in the body when the body can no longer work aerobically and anaerobic glycolysis occurs.

The two golden rules of developing the cardiovascular system are:

1. Reduce the production of lactate by having a higher aerobic threshold.

2. Increase the rate of lactate removal from the working muscles by having a functioning anaerobic system.

The first rule is about maximizing your aerobic threshold. The second rule is about maximizing your anaerobic threshold. Both need to be trained very differently, but maximizing both is key to maximizing the cardiovascular system.

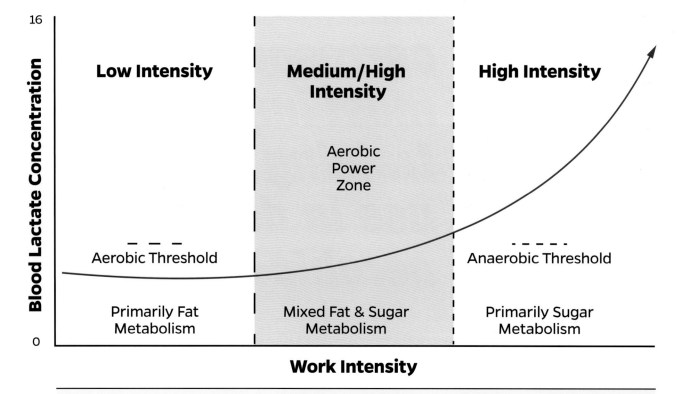

Blood Lactate Concentration

Low Intensity

Medium/High Intensity

High Intensity

Aerobic
Power
Zone

– – –
Aerobic Threshold

– – – –
Anaerobic Threshold

Primarily Fat
Metabolism

Mixed Fat & Sugar
Metabolism

Primarily Sugar
Metabolism

0

Work Intensity

FIGURE 2 - LACTATE AS MEASURE OF INTENSITY

Figure 2 illustrates where the aerobic threshold sits and how blood lactate concentration starts to increase as workout intensity increases. It also illustrates the body's primary fuel sources at each level.

As you can see in the image, there are essentially three zones of training: below the aerobic threshold, the Aerobic Power Zone, and above the anaerobic threshold.

One of the biggest problems we see with everyday athletes is that they don't spend time developing the aerobic or anaerobic threshold individually. Instead, they spend the vast majority of their time training in the Aerobic Power Zone that uses both glucose and fat for fuel.

The secret of the world's elite endurance athletes is that they have shrunk their Aerobic Power Zone and closed the gap between the aerobic threshold and the anaerobic threshold. Most elite endurance athletes have less than a 10% difference between the two thresholds. This means they can perform faster,

for longer, and more frequently working below their aerobic threshold, using fat stores as their primary fuel source.

Figure 3 illustrates an example of an advanced endurance athlete with a high aerobic base. Notice how they can work out harder, for longer, before blood lactate starts to accumulate. Their Aerobic Power Zone is much smaller so they spend less time using glucose (sugars) for energy and more time using fat.

On the flip side, **Figure 4** shows somebody who suffers from Aerobic Deficiency Syndrome (ADS). They have a very poor aerobic threshold, and their Aerobic Power Zone is considerably larger. This means they will tire much faster than the advanced athlete.

I would argue that the vast majority of the world's population suffers from ADS. We are so wired to believe that we should work intensely and harder, just like the sizzle reels of elite athlete training videos, that we often miss the hard work, dedication, and patience it requires to maximize true athletic potential.

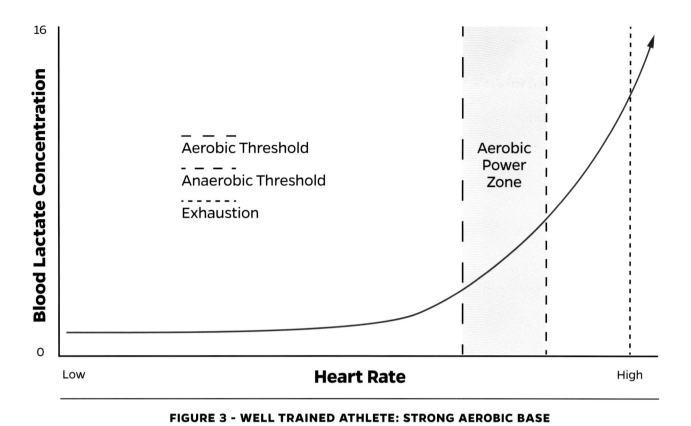

FIGURE 3 - WELL TRAINED ATHLETE: STRONG AEROBIC BASE

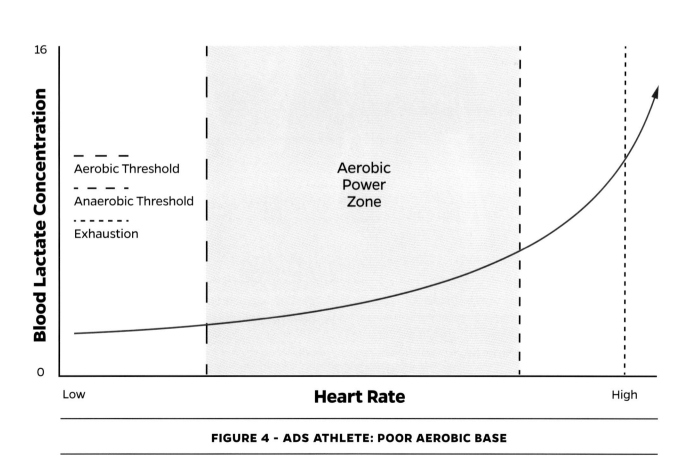

FIGURE 4 - ADS ATHLETE: POOR AEROBIC BASE

What Is Aerobic Deficiency Syndrome?

Aerobic Deficiency Syndrome (ADS) is one of the most common athletic issues we see in people who work with us for coaching and training. It's not a disease, so don't worry about that, but a term first coined by Dr. Phil Maffetone in the 1980s. It's a reversible condition that results from doing too much anaerobic or high-intensity exercise. People who exhibit it often have high-level anaerobic capacities from years of working out at these higher intensities. They feel athletic, fit, fast, and strong, but their aerobic base is completely underdeveloped, even non-existent. It means they have a huge Aerobic Power Zone, and are extremely good at exercising in this area, but cannot sustain base-level activity.

This condition can be devastating for endurance athletes since it contributes to reduced endurance. It leads to quickened fatigue, loss of aerobic speed, and overtraining. The first and most obvious sign of ADS is chronic fatigue. Chronic fatigue is typically due to the lack of aerobic base, resulting in greater reliance on glucose for energy—not just during workouts but at all other times of day and night. Another sign of ADS

is increased body fat. Less fat is used for energy and more remains stored throughout the body, which is also strongly associated with chronic inflammation.

Essentially, ADS means that the body is not as efficient as it should be. Typically heart rates are elevated, resulting in higher levels of stress. This not only affects athletes but everyday people too. Just think about it: the lower your aerobic threshold, the less energy you have throughout the day to complete routine tasks and the more time it takes you to recover from completing these tasks.

Having a high aerobic threshold allows you to perform more tasks, better and faster, and allows you to recover faster. As people move less and less, the harder these routine tasks become. Humans are becoming severely undertrained and are predominantly relying on their glucose levels to support them through the day. Can you see now why so many people reach for those sugary energy drinks daily?

How to Test Your Aerobic Threshold

Determining your aerobic threshold is THE MOST IMPORTANT FACTOR in developing your cardiovascular training and the base from which all other training plans and programs are written. So how do we test for your aerobic threshold? Remember, this is very different from testing your anaerobic threshold, so please don't get confused here.

The only true method of testing your aerobic threshold is performing a gas exchange test in a lab. There are very few labs around the world that can do this, and it is expensive to administer. I would say this test is for elite athletes only because, at the elite levels, the 1% differences count.

But for us mere mortals over thirty, we can use three simple methods:

1. The Talk Test
2. The Breath Test
3. Maximum Aerobic Function (MAF)

The warm-up for an elite athlete may completely overload a novice trainee, and what constitutes enough for one intermediate athlete may max out another.

1. The Talk Test

We ask people to perform some kind of cardiovascular exercise. If they cannot hold a normal conversation while performing this type of exercise, they are working above their aerobic threshold and need to slow down to continue working below their aerobic threshold.

2. The Breath Test

We ask people to perform some kind of cardiovascular exercise. While performing this type of exercise, if they cannot comfortably breathe through their nose while keeping their mouth closed, they are working above their aerobic threshold and need to slow down to continue working below their aerobic threshold.

We often ask people to perform this type of exercise with water held in their mouth to ensure nasal breathing is maintained throughout. That way we can ensure aerobic threshold training is maintained.

3. Maximum Aerobic Function

Maximum Aerobic Function (MAF) is our default and preferred method for aerobic threshold training and requires a heart rate monitor. Devised by Dr. Phil Maffetone in the 1980s, it is a simple formula of subtracting your age from 180.

Depending on your training history, Dr. Maffetone recommends the following modifications to the formula:

- **If you're recovering from an injury or get sick more than two to three times per year, subtract an additional five.**

- **If you've been training for more than two years and showing regular progress, then add five.**

Once you have determined your score, you then perform cardiovascular exercise at this intensity, or just below (no more than 10 beats below), but never above. It's not the perfect method, but for sake of simplicity and time-tested results with numerous world endurance champions, you can't go wrong with this method.

MAF Working Example:

Let's use me as an example. I'm 37 years old so 180 - 37 = 143

I have no history of illness or disease and have been training regularly for over two years. Therefore, I would add 5 beats. My final score is 148. Therefore, if I was performing cardiovascular exercise with the sole intent of improving my aerobic threshold, I would ensure my heart rate never exceeded 148. I would try to keep it between 138 and 148 to maximize the development of the aerobic threshold.

Training Working Example

Let's apply this to a training example: If I was to go for a 60 minute run, I would make sure to adhere to one of the following:

- **Running at a pace at which I can comfortably hold a conversation.**

- **Running at a pace at which I can comfortably breathe through my nose.**

- **Running at a pace at which my heart rate never exceeds 148 and never drops below 138.**

If at any time I couldn't adhere to any of these methods, I would simply slow down. Perhaps I would slow down so much that I would have to walk, which is a very common and regular occurrence when first applying this methodology. It's very different to training the anaerobic system. This is all about training well within your comfort zone.

How to Train to Maximize Your Aerobic Threshold

There's no easy way around this. The key to building your aerobic threshold is volume. Volume, volume, and more volume of sub-aerobic threshold training that allows us to build up our aerobic speed and make our movement economy more efficient in terms of technique and metabolism. We have to re-train the body to prioritize using fat as the primary fuel source for endurance-based activities, and that means spending hours and hours working out at below your aerobic threshold.

Remember, you will never maximize your cardiovascular potential without first maximizing your aerobic threshold. Having a robust aerobic system is paramount before we dive into developing your anaerobic threshold. A certain level of strength is required to allow us to go deep enough into this system to elicit the correct dose response. When we talk about volume, the question we always get asked is *"How much is enough?"*

A warm-up for an elite athlete may completely overload a novice trainee, and what constitutes enough for one intermediate athlete may completely overload another. When you work on building the aerobic threshold, there isn't a one-size-fits-all approach. It's unique to each individual in.

Your results will be directly proportional to the amount of work you put in, and building the cardiovascular engine and developing your aerobic threshold takes time, effort, and dedication. But I promise you, it's worth it in the long run.

If you want to build a truly robust aerobic threshold, you need to look at it from an annual training perspective and understand that volume and consistency is key to development. As a novice, you want to build to a minimum of 400 hours of training time each year working on the cardiovascular system, not including strength or movement-based workouts. That's roughly 7–8 hours a week dedicated to cardiovascular work.

At the top end, you're looking to build to 800+ hours of cardiovascular work each year. This is what the elite level men and women do, and it gives you an idea of what it takes to get to that level. You may be reading this and thinking I have no chance of hitting 400+ hours of training, let alone 800. You might be slightly deterred. I'm sorry to be the bearer of bad news, but this is what it takes to become a serious everyday athlete. Swinging a few kettlebells a few minutes each day or doing 10-minute booty blasts simply won't do.

Where to Start to Develop the Aerobic Threshold

If you've gasped at our 400 hours a year standard, please don't be intimidated. It wasn't put here to frighten you. It can easily be achieved if you have the right mindset and build a lifestyle around that mindset.

For beginners, the first step to building your aerobic threshold is to walk more. It really is that simple. Walk more. Walk to work. Go for evening strolls. Go for weekend hikes. Hit your 10k steps a day. For most people, this is the very best way to start, and it's the safest. If you're new to aerobic training, you can't jump into running 400+ hours a year if you've never run a single hour. You have to build up to it. Safety and longevity first. Once you have built up your walking abilities, maybe start to introduce run-walks. In the gym, choose the rower and assault bike over free-weights from time to time. Try and build up to 60 minutes of continuous work that adheres to the talk test, breath test, or MAF methods described earlier.

If you've gasped at our 400 hours a year standard, please don't be intimidated. It wasn't put here to frighten you. It can easily be achieved if you have the right mindset and build a lifestyle around that mindset.

For intermediate and advanced athletes, embrace the MAF method. Build your engine on long slow runs, keeping below your MAF heart rate. It is highly likely you suffer from ADS, which means the pace of your runs and rowing will be frustratingly slow! I know exactly how you will feel –embarrassed and like it's a waste of time. But trust me, stick with it. Elite marathon runners can run sub 5-minute miles below the aerobic threshold for mile after mile. Doing aerobic threshold work does not automatically mean going slow. Far from it. You just have to earn the right to build it. And it takes time, lots of it. But keep at it, and you really will start to train like an elite athlete. Aerobic threshold training makes up approximately 85% of their total annual training plans.

Why? Because they know what you don't. You need to build a solid foundation for the rest of your cardiovascular system. And that foundation is aerobic speed. Give it time. You will thank me later. You can also join the Strength Matters online support group of training members in the low heart rate training group.

What is the Anaerobic Threshold?

If you don't maximally develop your aerobic energy system first and have sufficient levels of strength, you will never truly maximize your anaerobic threshold.

Understanding the Anaerobic Threshold

The anaerobic threshold is the lowest intensity of exercise at which the production of lactate exceeds the body's ability to utilize lactate as fuel in aerobic metabolism. Once you go above this intensity, blood lactate levels begin to rise. The greater the intensity of exercise above the anaerobic threshold, the greater the rise in blood lactate as the production of lactate exceeds its rate of removal. Exercising above the anaerobic threshold can only be sustained for a few minutes at a time before fatigue sets in, causing you to slow down.

In simple terms, this is the maximum amount of work you can sustain for a long duration. Your pace at anaerobic threshold is the greatest predictor of endurance performance because it is the rate at which the body can sustainably produce energy. Every athlete knows this point. You know you can only hold this pace for a short time before you have to stop. That's your anaerobic threshold.

It's important to understand the role of lactic acid, which is so often seen as the cause of poor cardiovascular capacity. Lactic acid only appears in the body when the body can no longer work aerobically and anaerobic glycolysis occurs.

> **Let's remind ourselves of the two golden rules of developing the cardiovascular system:**
>
> 1. Reduce the production of lactate by having a higher aerobic threshold.
>
> 2. Increase the rate of lactate removal from the working muscles by having a fully functioning anaerobic system.

Step 1 is all about maximizing your aerobic threshold. Step 2 is about maximizing your anaerobic threshold. Both need to be trained very differently, but both are key to maximizing the cardiovascular system.

With that logic in mind, I would argue even more strongly that over 90% of the world's population has no right to train the anaerobic threshold. As you now know through the Strength Matters Hierarchy of Athletic Development, there is a logic and process to truly maximize your cardiovascular potential.

Anaerobic threshold development is the last component.

What Is the Difference Between Anaerobic Threshold and Lactate Threshold?

Anaerobic threshold and lactate threshold can both represent the maximum pace sustainable for an extended duration. We choose to use the term anaerobic threshold as it is in keeping with our ideas of aerobic threshold development, and it keeps the language consistent between coaches and athletes.

To everyone except sport scientists, these terms are interchangeable. The key difference is that lactate threshold is determined by measuring the amount of lactate in the athlete's blood during a lab test, rather than measuring oxygen consumed for the anaerobic threshold. Either way, when the lactate volume in the blood reaches around 4mmol/L (millimoles per litre), the athlete is assumed to be at lactate or anaerobic threshold.

Why Is Your Anaerobic Threshold Important?

From a cardiovascular endurance performance standpoint, the ability to make use of lactate in the muscles as fuel is one of the most important training adaptations you can make as an athlete. This is why having a strong, robust anaerobic system is important to maximizing your cardiovascular potential. Once you have maximized your aerobic threshold, which focuses on reducing the rate at which lactate is produced, you can then focus on improving the body's ability to remove it.

The best way to view your cardiovascular system is to think of it as a vacuum, which sucks up all the lactate. The greater the aerobic threshold, the bigger the vacuum. The bigger the capacity of the vacuum, the more the anaerobic system can contribute to the overall energy production within the body.

The greater the aerobic threshold, the bigger the vacuum.

The more robust and trained the anaerobic system is, the MORE powerful the vacuum becomes, thus sucking up lactate at a much faster rate, allowing you to perform faster and for longer.

This is why you can never fully maximize your cardiovascular potential, no matter how high the intensity of the exercise you do, if you don't fully develop your aerobic threshold first. Your vacuum simply isn't big enough to hold all the lactate the body produces. It's like trying to put a V8 engine inside a smart car. The key to maximal cardiovascular development is combining both aerobic threshold development and anaerobic threshold development.

Once you have maximized your aerobic threshold, which focuses on reducing the rate at which lactate is produced, you can then focus on improving the body's ability to remove it.

Here's what makes this type of training an art form. It's more than just science and it depends on each individual athlete or person. Increasing the aerobic threshold requires a high volume of low intensity exercise, whereas improving the anaerobic threshold requires high intensity exercise. The key takeaway is this: you need far less anaerobic threshold training than you think. We suggest for everyday athletes over thirty, 90% of your annual training volume needs to be aerobic threshold training based in nature. That's right, only 10% of your annual training plan needs to be anaerobic in nature to maximize your cardiovascular potential.

Have You Earned the Right to Train Your Anaerobic Threshold?

I've said this before, and I'll say it again:

If you don't maximally develop your aerobic energy system first and have sufficient levels of strength, you will never truly maximize your anaerobic threshold.

But what constitutes enough strength and a robust aerobic energy system?

To elicit the correct dose-response from anaerobic training, you need to dig deep into your central nervous system. This only comes with significant pre-requisite strength and aerobic capacity. Here are our minimum strength standards that must be met prior to training the anaerobic threshold:

Women

- **1.25 x bodyweight deadlift x 5 reps**

- **Bodyweight back squat x 5 reps**

- **3 x pull-ups**

- **3 x dips**

- **75% bodyweight farmers carry - 90 seconds**

Men

- **1.5 x bodyweight deadlift x 5 reps · Bodyweight back squat x 5 reps**

- **5 x pull-ups**

- **5 x dips**

- **75% bodyweight farmers carry - 90 seconds**

In addition to these strength standards, everyday athletes must demonstrate a strong aerobic threshold. To determine this, our go-to test follows.

Men/Women

- **Can you run 10km in under 60 minutes with your heart rate below MAF (180 - Age) at all times?**

Can you now see why we believe 90% of the world's population shouldn't be doing anaerobic threshold work? If you can't achieve these baseline standards, we do not recommend anaerobic threshold training for you.

Anaerobic threshold work is for advanced athletes, not beginners. It's why anaerobic capacity is a Layer 3 component on the Strength Matters Hierarchy of Athletic Development. It's also why anaerobic work doesn't appear until Phase Three of the training plan in this book. You have to develop the right to truly maximize your cardiovascular potential.

Aerobic Battery

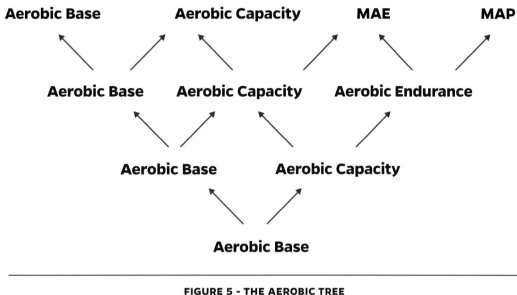

FIGURE 5 - THE AEROBIC TREE

How to Train to Maximize Your Anaerobic Threshold

Before I talk to you about how to train anaerobic threshold, I want to introduce you to the Aerobic Tree, our model for developing aerobic capacity. I want to highlight the fact that there is much work ahead of you before you earn the right to train anaerobically, in our humble opinion. Yet, many people skip nearly all of this foundational work.

At the base of the tree, you have your Aerobic Base. This is as simple as walking 10,000 steps a day. As you climb the tree, you add layers to your development. Next is Aerobic Capacity - the ability to do continuous exercise for at least 60 minutes. Once we have the base and can achieve 60 minutes of continuous work, we want to become as efficient as possible at completing these 60 minute pieces. It may be even longer.

Marathon runners may not run as fast as 100m sprinters, but they still run fast comparatively. It's something to think about before you dismiss aerobic work.

Then, and only once we become extremely proficient in these 60 minute pieces, can we climb to the top of the tree and perform **MAE (Maximal Aerobic Endurance)**, the ability to extend out to hours and hours of work, and **MAP (Maximal Aerobic Power)** work. MAP is the sexy, fun work in aerobic capacity. These are aerobic threshold and power intervals that get faster and faster in nature. This isn't something you can jump into straight away. You need base work, basic aerobic capacity and aerobic endurance, in place first so that you can recover quickly to perform each working set.

Aerobic does not automatically mean slow in nature, which is what most people think. Elite marathoners run sub-5 minute miles for 26.1 miles straight. There aren't many people who can run one mile at that pace, let alone 26.1. Marathon runners may not run as fast as 100m sprinters, but they still run fast comparatively. It's something to think about before you dismiss aerobic work.

How Do I Increase My Anaerobic Threshold?

You have to earn the right to train your anaerobic threshold. You need to have the pre-requisite strength levels, and you must have progressed all the way through the aerobic tree.

Here are the key concepts to remember as we progress:

· **Aerobic Capacity:** train from Endurance to Power

· **Anaerobic Capacity:** You train from Power to Endurance

The basic principles of anaerobic threshold training are:

1. Train intervals to exhaustion

2. Rest completely

3. Repeat

There is one caveat: all intervals must be identical in nature. This means that what you do is repeatable until it is not. It is when these intervals are no longer sustainable that you either stop for the day or, in the next session, you progress your workload.

The anaerobic system needs to be fully restored for each interval so that you can train to the same maximum intensity. Work periods tend to be short, sometimes as little as 8 seconds, separated by long recovery times. If the rest period is too short, the workout will shift to endurance training. The energy system you are training needs to fully recover to elicit the correct dose response. As a general rule of thumb, our resting protocols tend to be around 10:1 (rest ten times the amount of work that you put in).

There is one caveat: all intervals must be identical in nature. This means that what you do is repeatable until it is not. It is when these intervals are no longer sustainable that you either stop for the day or, in the next session, you progress your workload.

How to Improve Anaerobic Endurance

Anaerobic and endurance. Maybe you're thinking these two words shouldn't go together. How can anaerobic work, which is unsustainable in nature, be considered endurance?

Well, they do go together. There's no easy way, this type of training is hard. Very hard. It hurts.

Improving your anaerobic threshold requires maximum training at the maximum intensity and then extending the time at which you perform it over a longer period.

For example, progressing 10 second sprints for ten sets (identical) to 14 seconds sprints for ten sets (identical). Unlike aerobic threshold work, anaerobic training requires us to produce as much lactate as possible and to maintain that high level for as long as possible before giving ample rest to allow the body to remove the lactate.

This is how we train the body to get better at removing lactate from the body. It's exhausting work, and it is why you need years and years of training behind you before even attempting it. More importantly, if you have earned the right to train like this, anaerobic threshold work should only make up 10% of your annual training volume. You need far, far less of this and far, far more of aerobic threshold work than you think.

Training the anaerobic threshold is one of the most misunderstood aspects of training the cardiovascular system. It is fashionable to train, as popularized by the world of HIIT. However, as you have now learned, it takes years and years of work and dedication to actually earn the right to train the anaerobic system if you are truly looking to maximize your athletic potential. A strong aerobic base and pre-requisite levels of strength are paramount before attempting this type of training. Anaerobic work appears in phase three of this training plan, however, you have to make the decision whether or not you have earned the right to complete phase three. That decision is down to you alone.

The key to training the anaerobic threshold is less volume, higher intensity, and progression from power to endurance. There are no shortcuts, and there is no easy way out. Either way, you have to decide whether you're eligible to progress.

STRENGTH
MATTERS®

MADE FOR LIFE

This program has allowed me to break boundaries, release limitations and given me freedom to do more, be more and enjoy more.

Geni Ligday, Everyday Athlete.

Personal Training. It's Like Being Stuck In 1999.

Train anywhere. Train on your schedule. Get better results. Online personal coaching with Strength Matters will allow you to reclaim precious lost hours each week. Allowing you to train more frequently for faster results. Start your coaching journey today.

Visit **www.strengthmatters.com.**

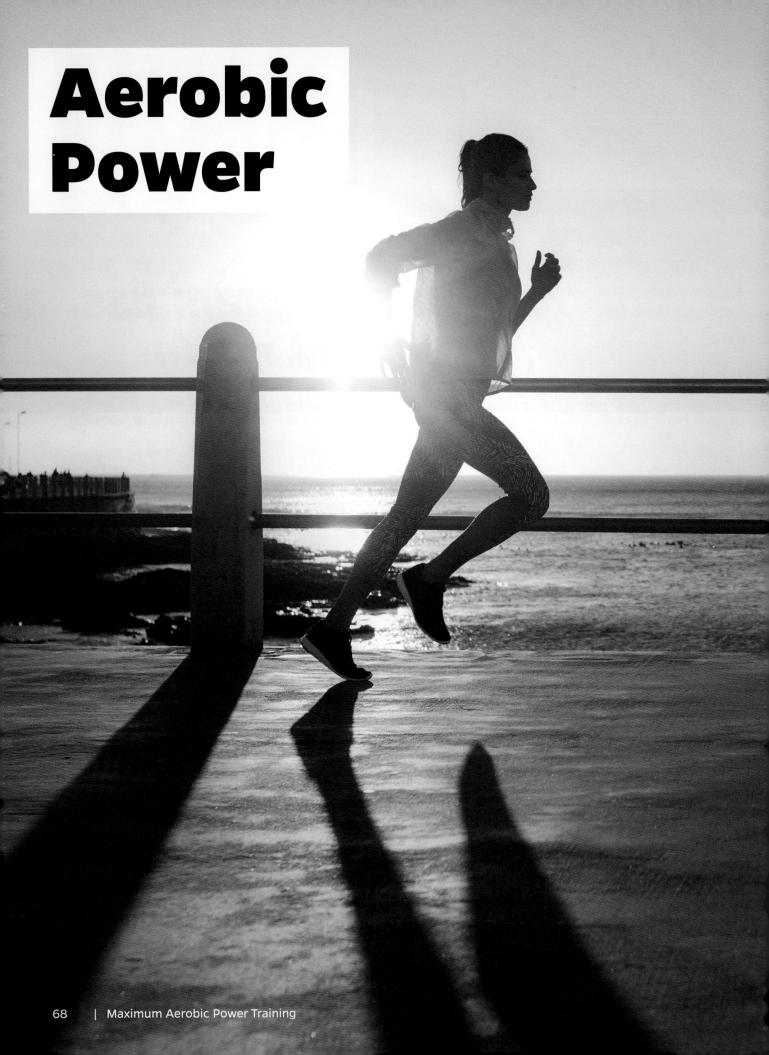

Aerobic
Power

Now that you understand our principles and philosophy of cardiovascular training, and know the differences between the aerobic and anaerobic thresholds, the question that often comes up is:

Can I train the Aerobic Power Zone?

The answer to this is a relatively straight forward 100% yes. You need to train the Aerobic Power Zone.

Your Body is Like a Car

Imagine your body is a car. It has five gears. To get the most out of the car's performance and to prolong its lifespan, you need to be able to use the full range of gears, one through five. You need to use the right gear, at the right time, at the right speed.

First and second gears are all about that explosive start. It's like the alactic and lactic energy systems using all that stored energy to get you up to 50 mph as fast as possible. It's that short, sharp explosive burst. Fifth gear is cruise control. This is the aerobic energy system kicking in, allowing you to be as efficient as possible at 60+ mph to cover those long miles you're putting in on the road. Gears three to four assist the process in getting you from one to five, and five to one respectfully. These gears also serve a purpose.

Dependant on terrain, road conditions and speed, they have their unique merits.

Most of the everyday athletes over thirty that we work with are stuck between gears three and four. They don't have the prerequisite strength levels to express themselves explosively in gears one and two, or the aerobic capacity to recover quickly or to do this repeatedly when required. Conversely, they don't have the efficiency or engine robustness to work in gear five for prolonged periods of time.

If we're not using the full five gears, we're not working optimally, and if we're not working optimally, we run the risk of breaking down. Understanding this analogy is imperative to applying our system of cardiovascular development.

Comparing the Gears of a Car to Heart Rate Training Zones

Our analogy of a car, is the perfect way to introduce you to the concept of heart rate training zones. The only difference is that Zone 1 in heart training is like fifth gear, and Zone 5 is like first gear. Just be aware of that as we progress.

ZONE 5
90-100%   ANAEROBIC THRESHOLD

ZONE 4
80-90%   AEROBIC POWER

ZONE 3
70-80%   AEROBIC POWER

ZONE 2
60-70%   AEROBIC THRESHOLD

ZONE 1
50-60%   AEROBIC THRESHOLD

Heart Rate Training Zones

Heart rate-based training uses your heart rate in beats per minute (bpm) or a percentage of your maximum heart rate as a guide for intensity. So instead of training at a specific pace, you can use these zones and a heart rate monitor to ensure your cardiovascular system is working at a specific effort for a set amount of time.

The idea behind heart rate-based training is to train your aerobic system without overstressing your central nervous, skeletal, or muscular systems. By working out in each heart rate zone, you're holding yourself back from pushing too hard, which can help you avoid overtraining. And since your maximum heart rate is unique to you, using it to create training zones means you're getting a much more personalized workout.

Looking at heart rate training in terms of aerobic and anaerobic thresholds, Zone 1 and Zone 2 will classify as aerobic threshold work (fifth gear) and Zone 5 as anaerobic threshold work (gears one and two). This leaves the remaining Zones 3 and 4. In the broadest of terms, these zones fall into the middle zone of training which we are now about to unravel.

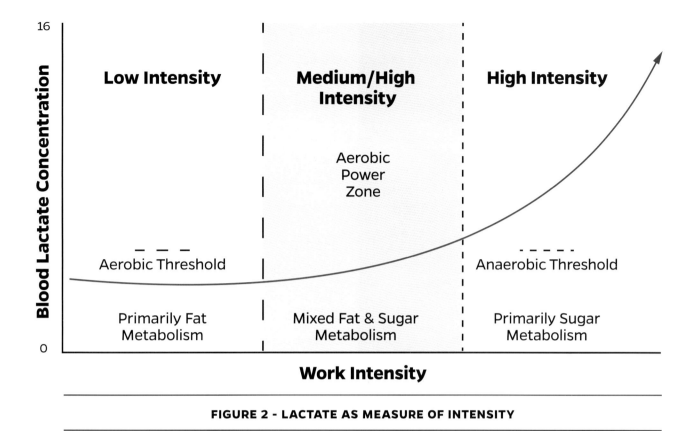

FIGURE 2 - LACTATE AS MEASURE OF INTENSITY

Figure 2 is here to serve as a reminder of the Aerobic Power Zone we're referring to.

In order to understand the Aerobic Power Zone you need to remind yourself of the two golden rules of developing the cardiovascular system:

1. Reduce the production of lactate by having a higher aerobic threshold.

2. Increase the rate of lactate removal from the working muscles by having a fully functioning anaerobic system.

This means we first want to maximize your aerobic threshold and then, we concentrate on maximizing your anaerobic threshold. Both need to be trained very differently, but both are key to developing the cardiovascular system. The Aerobic Power Zone bridges the gap between the two and helps to prepare the body for the strenuous work required for anaerobic threshold development.

Developing the cardiovascular system has three distinct phases. Irrespective of age and ability, we always start with low intensity aerobic threshold work and focus on building volume. We then progress to Aerobic Power, and then finally, Anaerobic Threshold work.

Phase One: Aerobic Threshold

Aerobic threshold work is where we like to start things off. In terms of training zones, it's Zones 1 and 2. In car terms, it's fifth gear. We need to train the body to become as efficient as possible.

Volume, consistency, and low intensity work is key to this process. Later down the line, it will allow us to recover faster and enable us to go deeper into the central nervous system to elicit the correct response from harder, more anaerobic workouts. The body reacts to stress differently, and we want to work in conjunction with the central nervous system so it doesn't freak out when we start to ramp up the stress later in our training.

The brain has one job: To keep us alive. Therefore, we need to respect and obey the laws of the nervous system. People often ask how much is enough low-intensity work? At what point am I able to progress to the next stage? Simply put, you can't get enough low intensity work. It's always, and should always be, a staple of your annual training plan - at least 90% of it. However, we do have a baseline test that allows us to see if the body is ready and able to progress to the next stage, and that is the 10 km run MAF test.

Can you run 10 km in under 60 minutes with your heart rate below MAF at all times?

If someone is able to perform this test, and is ideally closer to the 50 minute mark, we know we have a robust everyday athlete who's ready to handle the rigors of more aerobic power training and anaerobic work. The sad reality of this test is that most people struggle on their first attempt to do it in under 1 hour and 20 minutes. Anything over the 60 minute mark in our eyes is the sign of someone who suffers from ADS (Aerobic Deficiency Syndrome) and is not moving as economically as they should be.

There's no getting away from this, Phase One training takes time and effort. But if you invest wisely during this phase of your training cycle, you will reap the benefits for years to come.

Phase Two: Aerobic Power Zone

This phase is the gateway to anaerobic threshold training, which as we now know is one of the secrets to endurance training. As we progress into the Aerobic Power Zone, our engine is now dropping down through the gears. We're moving from fifth gear to gears four and three, increasing our rate of power production as we do. Coincidently, it is the same as if we view this in terms of heart rate training zones. This is Zones 3 and 4, respectively.

This aside, because we have a lot of time building up a robust aerobic system, we can spend more time training these zones because our ability to recover will be that much faster. If we can recover faster, we can do more volume with a slightly reduced risk of injury. Remember, fatigue plays a big part in injury risk. And if we're playing by the rules of the brain and the central nervous system, we've earned the right to push the body a little bit harder. We've raised the comfort level, but not by much. We still have a long way to go before we can even consider pure anaerobic work.

The rules of the Aerobic Power Zone are about repeatability of the work performed. We are now moving from training endurance into power. This means we're going from long slow sustained work to shorter, sharper, faster contractions of work that are repeatable in nature. For example, if you complete a 400 m lap in 1 minute and 27 seconds, further repeats of the 400m lap must be 1:27 also.

In this phase, as the pace of work progresses from slower to much faster, we are progressing from aerobic threshold work to aerobic power. Interval training becomes our default method for training this zone. In terms of heart rate zones, this will be performed above your MAF calculation (180 - age), Zones 3 and 4 essentially, but below Zone 5. The method of

progression is then to add volume of training, then increasing the pace of that volume of training. That right there is the secret to Aerobic Power Zone training, which sets you up for phase three - anaerobic threshold specific work.

Phase Three: Anaerobic Threshold

I might have said this enough times already, but, I'm going to say it again for good measure, just in case you skipped everything else in the book:

If you don't maximally develop your aerobic energy system first and have sufficient levels of strength, you will never truly maximize your anaerobic threshold.

This is the phase everyone likes to skip to, the high intensity workouts that leave you a sweating heap on the floor. This is first and second gear in terms of the car analogy we used, and Zone 5 in terms of heart rate zones. To elicit the correct response from anaerobic training, you need to be able to dig deep into your central nervous system. This only comes with significant prerequisite strength and aerobic capacity. We talked about this in great depth earlier in the book, in the anaerobic threshold chapter, so I won't re-visit it here.

I would argue that for everyday athletes over thirty, it would take years to get to this level of intense training if they followed the protocols we laid out above. This means spending a significant amount of time in phase one, working the aerobic threshold, and then spending an equally significant amount of time in phase two, the middle zone of aerobic power. This is five to ten years of work for some people or, for the more advanced, maybe a year at the earliest. Either way, it takes time to truly develop maximum physical potential and we can't fast track the body.

Training the anaerobic system works in stark contrast to training the aerobic system, where we train endurance first then train in the direction of power. The opposite is true for anaerobic threshold training: power development comes first and then we develop anaerobic endurance

Maximum Aerobic Power Training

Training the Aerobic Power Zone is an incredibly important aspect of training the cardiovascular system. It bridges the gap between the aerobic and anaerobic thresholds, and is the gateway to anaerobic training performance. In the vast majority of cases, people only ever live in this phase of training, not even realizing other cardio training zones exist, and certainly not knowing they don't have the levels of strength or aerobic capacity needed to even elicit the correct response for anaerobic training.

Looking at this middle zone through the lens of heart rate training, this means people skip training Zones 1 and 2, and jump straight into Zones 3, 4, and 5. In terms of a car's gear system, they are not using the full range of gears available to them, which means they won't be performing optimally, and you can forget about the notion of longevity.

Imagine for a minute not having first, second, and fifth gear in a car. What would that do to your life and your car? Cause havoc, right? It takes hours of work and dedication to earn the right to train this middle zone and aerobic power system. A strong aerobic base and prerequisite levels of strength are paramount before even attempting this type of training - similar to that of anaerobic threshold training.

over time. We want to train anaerobically for three main reasons: stress adaptation, the metabolic effect, and to boost the aerobic system.

However, Phase Three anaerobic training becomes irrelevant if you don't first have enough strength to elicit the desired effect of this type of training. You will not be able to release enough stored energy to a degree that makes this type of training meaningful. You will recover far too quickly and will not push your central nervous system hard enough.

Conversely, if you are strong enough, but don't have enough aerobic capacity and endurance, you will not have enough energy in the tank to progress far enough into the anaerobic development system. You simply need both. This is why an intelligent training plan that combines both strength and aerobic capacity is necessary to bring you up to this point.

The key to training the middle zone is repeatability of the work performed and the progression from training endurance into power. This means we're going from slow sustained work into faster contractions of work that is repeatable in nature. Stick with these rules, and you'll build a powerful, robust aerobic engine the right way.

Part Two

Recommended Training Equipment

We recommend the following equipment and products to help get the most from your Maximum Aerobic Power Training Program.

- **Cast Iron Kettlebells**

- **Heart Rate Monitor**

- **Concept 2 Rowing Machine**

- **Assault Bike**

- **Wall Balls/Medicine Balls**

- **Pull-Up Bar**

- **TRX/Rings**

- **Running Shoes**

- **Barbell + Plates**

- **Athletic Track**

- **Foam Roller**

Pre-requisite Fitness Standards

Prior to attempting the Maximum Aerobic Power Training Program, we recommend that you have the following baseline movement, strength, and cardio standards in place.

5 Minute Deep Squat Sit:

This standard is all about good hip flexion and ankle dorsiflexion and adequate levels of thoracic spine extension. This is a foundational requirement prior to attempting this training plan. If not, your risk of injury will be heightened and your athletic development will be hindered.

30 Second Balance on One Leg, Eyes Closed:

Standing barefoot with hands out to the side and your eyes closed, attempt to stand on one leg without falling over or losing balance. This test is all about the health of your vestibular system and proprioceptive feedback under foot.

2 Minute Straight Arm Plank Test:

Hold a straight arm plank for 2 minutes. If you are unable to hold this, you need to develop your core strength prior to attempting this training plan. This is our baseline foundational strength test, and it must be passed prior to commencing any other type of training.

5 Rep Bodyweight Deadlift:

Like the two-minute plank, this is foundational strength work, and your body will not be able to tolerate the workload of the program if this cannot be achieved.

5 Rep Bodyweight Back Squat

Like the two-minute plank and deadlift, this is foundational strength work and your body will not be able to tolerate the workload of the program if this standard cannot be achieved.

30 Minute Continuous Run

This program contains an element of running. It is highly recommended that you are able to run continuously for at least 30 minutes prior to commencing this program. If you have never run before or haven't participated in running for a long time, we would recommend building up to this achievement. Statistically, running is one of the most injury-ridden sports in the world. It is not something you should jump into straight away.

Phase 1:
Build The Engine

Build the Engine Training

Lay the foundation.

Duration: 6-18 weeks.

Goals

1. Complete each workout A, B, and C for the full 45 minutes and hit all the prescribed sets and reps in the given time frame.

2. Run continuously, without stopping for 60-minutes at MAF heart rate as a recovery day.

3. Change in mindset and adapt to a training schedule of seven days a week.

Build the Engine Schedule

Your training will consist of six days a week training and will include one active rest day. Workouts will last no more than 60-minutes and some will be as short as 25 minutes. Depending on your skill levels this program should last between 6-18 weeks; as you can accomplish the required goals, then the volume and intensity will increase. If it feels easy to begin with, don't push it. We're working in conjunction with the central nervous systemhere. It will soon get hard, trust me.

Choose your weights accordingly. Only you can decide what is right for you and your body. From experience, it's better to err on the lighter side than have to drop down in weight mid-set. You will need to go lighter than you think.

Mon	Tue	Wed	Thu	Fri	Sat	Sun
A	WR	B	WR	C	WR	H

As you can see the schedule consists of an A/B/C split with a sandwich of Walk/Run sessions and a hiking day. The workouts will remain the same. The intensity and volume will change with each workout. Your body will dictate what you do on the Walk/Run days. These days are meant to be easy in nature and only you can decide the intensity at which you perform them. **Volume here is more important than the intensity.**

Equipment

For this phase of training, you will need the following pieces of equipment:

1. **Kettlebells (in pairs)**

2. **Wallballs or Medicine Balls**

3. **Concept 2 Rowing Machine (or equivalent)**

4. **Running Shoes**

5. **A pull-up bar**

6. **Assault Bike**

7. **TRX or Gymnastic Rings**

Warm Up: 5-10 Minutes

Prior to all training sessions, we recommend completing a thorough warm-up. At Strength Matters we believe in an individualized approach to warm-ups; however, for the nature of this training plan, we have provided a list of sample mobility exercises you can complete before each workout.

Mobility exercises we like to use regularly include:

1. **Diaphragmatic Breathing**

2. **Quadruped Neck Nods and Rotations**

3. **Quadruped Cat Cow**

4. **Quadruped Thoracic Rotation**

5. **Downward Dog/Upward Dog**

6. **Half-kneeling Kettlebell Halos**

7. **Goblet Squats with Prying to loosen the hips**

8. **Deep Squat Sit with Overhead Reach**

9. **Cossack Hip Openers**

10. **Foam Rolling**

The most important thing is to take the time to mobilize thoroughly. Never underestimate the power of a good warm-up and the importance it plays going into your workout.

Activation Work: 5-10 Minutes

This is a non-negotiable element of this training plan. All workouts must begin with activation work. Activation work is defined by purposeful movements that activate both the nervous and muscular systems. We stimulate neurological pathways of the nervous system that will either directly or indirectly help with the planned movements for the main workout.

The muscles that we are most concerned with activating are the stabilizer muscles, which are necessary for efficient force production during the main workout. To keep things simple, you will perform the following activation work prior to each of the three core workouts.

Perform 3 rounds. No rest.

A1 Single Arm Overhead Kettlebell Squat (Light weight) - 5/5 reps

A2 Hanging Knee Leg Raise - 5 reps

A3 Half-Kneeling Kettlebell Windmill - 5/5 reps

A4 Leopard Crawl - 10 Steps Forwards/10 Steps Backwards

Repeat.

Stretch: 2-10 Minutes

We believe that all everyday athletes should stretch for 5-10 minutes at the end of every training session (unless in a rare circumstance, such as hyper-mobility). Post-workout stretching, while the soft tissue is warm and malleable, will offer faster improvements.

We have three basic stretching principles:

1. **Diaphragmatic breathing is fundamental to increasing range of motion**

2. **Contract-relax stretching trumps static stretching**

3. **Any stretch should take a minimum of 2 minutes**

We understand that most people skip this portion of the workout; however, do so at your peril. If you are lacking time, we recommend focusing on one area and doing that one area well!

Here is a list of stretching exercises we would recommend using during phase 1:

1. **The Bretzel**

2. **The Couch/Tree Stretch**

3. **Banded Hamstring Work (lying down)**

4. **90:90 Stretch**

5. **Pigeon Stretch**

Workout A

Workout A - Notes

500m Rowing Pace

Row with your feet out of the straps. This is for efficiency of transfer from one exercise to another and a skill based drill to improve your rowing leg drive.

Choose a pace that is sustainable and repeatable in nature. This means each 500m row time must be identical.

Your pace shouldn't fluctuate. If you can't hit the same pace for each set, you haven't earned the right to progress. This is a skill in itself.

For example, a correct set should read 2:12, 2:12, 2:12, etc.

If it reads 2:02, 1:57, 2:12, etc., this is not correct, and you need to spend time practicing the skill of repeated sets.

The pace you choose should be easy. At the end of the workout, you should feel that you could continue going for another 60 minutes. If not, slow down next time.

Not sure what pace to start with, our suggestion:

Men: 2:16

Women: 2:26

Adjust accordingly up or down until all working sets are identical in nature.

Wall Ball Thrusters

This is not a contest to see how much weight you can throw. This is a speed-strength drill. Choose a light weight that you can throw and catch. Do not drop the ball. Aim for a 10-foot marker. The final set should feel just as easy as the first set. If you can't complete all 10 reps for the duration, you've gone too heavy.

Weight suggestions:

Men: 8lb-20lb medicine ball

Women: 5lb-14lb medicine ball

Single Arm Kettlebell Swings

Again, this is not a weight or grip contest. This is more about the movement than anything else. Choose a light to medium weight that you can swing comfortably single handed. Perform 5 reps on one side, then switch effortlessly to the opposite side and perform another 5 reps. As soon as you've completed the swings, immediately return to the rower and repeat the circuit.

Weight suggestions:

Men: 16kg-32kg kettlebell
Women: 8kg-20kg kettlebell

The 1:15 Time Frame

This is important. You will have sufficient time to complete the wall balls and swings with a few seconds to spare to allow you to begin rowing before the countdown ends.

It's all about the transition from exercise to exercise and working continuously. This is why rowing with your feet out of the straps is a must. If you can't keep pace, it suggests you do not have the pre-requisite conditioning skills to perform this workout. If that's the case, increase the resting time and work your way down so that you can complete the full 20-minutes at this intensity.

The Progression

The progression of this workout is simple. I didn't say easy. I said simple. Once you can complete 20-minutes comfortably, you simply increase the time by 5-minutes each workout, up to a total of 45 minutes.

It could look like this:
Week 1: 20 Minutes
Week 2: 25 Minutes
Week 3: 30 Minutes
Week 4: 35 Minutes
Week 5: 40 Minutes
Week 6: 45 Minutes

However, the rules when you increase are as follows:

1. Your row time remains exactly the same. For example, if you rowed in 2:12 each set during the first 20 minutes, you continue rowing at 2:12. You do not increase or decrease the pace.

2. You must complete all sets and reps of wall ball thrusters and kettlebell swings.

3. The 1:15 rest period remains a constant.

The final 45-minute workout could look like this:

WORKOUT A - 45 MINUTE EXAMPLE

A1 500m Row at 2:12
A2 Wall Ball Thrusters (Light) x 10
A3 Single Arm KB Swing (Light/Medium) x 5/5

Repeat for the full 45 minutes. No rest between any exercise.

Set the rower for 500m intervals with 1:15 rest.

*Wallballs and swings to be completed in the 1:15 resting time.

At the end of the workout, you should feel that you could continue going for another 60 minutes.

Workout B

Warm-Up
Activation Exercises
Workout:

Total workout time 20 minutes.

A1 15 Kcal Assault Bike
A2 25% Max Push-Ups
A3 15Kcal Assault Bike
A4 25% Max TRX/Ring Rows

Repeat. No Rest.

* Each 15kcal is EXACTLY THE SAME split time. For example, 2:00 for each. If you cannot maintain pace, slow down!

You should feel at the end of the workout that you could continue going for another 60 minutes.

Stretch

Workout B - Notes

Assault Bike Pace

Choose a pace that is sustainable and repeatable in nature. This means each 15kcal must be identical in time. **Your pace shouldn't fluctuate.** If you can't hit the same pace for each set, you haven't earned the right to progress. This is a skill in itself.

For example, a correct set could read 2:00, 2:00, 2:00, etc.

If it reads 2:02, 1:57, 2:12, etc., this is not correct, and you need to spend time practicing the skill of intra set repeatability. The pace you choose should be easy in nature. At the end of the workout, you should feel that you could continue going for another 60 minutes. If not, slow down next time.

Not sure what time to start with, our suggestion:

Men: 2:00
Women: 2:10

Adjust accordingly up or down until all working sets are identical in nature.

I Don't Have an Assault Bike
It's not uncommon for people not to have access to an assault bike. If this is the case, switch to a concept 2 rower.

25% Max Push-Ups

Prior to starting this workout, ideally on a separate day when you are not fatigued, perform a max push-up test. Each push-up should be performed at a 31x1 tempo (3 seconds down, 1 second pause, explode up, 1 second pause). Good push-up form and technique is recommended. We suggest going low enough so that your nose can almost touch the floor. During the workout, you'll only be performing 25% of your max effort. That's a 1:4 ratio.

Working example:
Max Push-up test = 20 reps
Rep scheme during workout B = 5 reps

25% Max TRX/Ring Rows

Prior to starting this workout, ideally on a separate day when you are not fatigued, perform a max ring-row test. Each TRX/ring row should be performed at a 31x1 tempo (3 seconds down, 1 second pause, explode up, 1 second pause). Good row form and technique is recommended. During the workout, you'll only be performing 25% of your max effort.

Working example:
Max TRX/Ring Row Test = 28 reps
Rep scheme during workout B = 7 reps

The Progression

The progression of this workout is identical to Workout A. Once you can complete 20 minutes comfortably, you simply increase the time by 5 minutes each workout, up to a total of 45 minutes.

It could look like this:

Week 1: 20 Minutes

Week 2: 25 Minutes

Week 3: 30 Minutes

Week 4: 35 Minutes

Week 5: 40 Minutes

Week 6: 45 Minutes

However, the rules when you increase are as follows:

1. Your assault bike time remains exactly the same. For example, if you did 15Kcal in 2:00 each set during the first 20 minutes, you continue at 2:00. You do not increase or decrease the pace.

2. You must complete all 25% sets and reps of push-ups and TRX/ring rows. If you cannot, you have not earned the right to progress in time.

3. At the end of each workout, you should feel that you could continue going for another 60 minutes. If not, you're going too fast. This should be easy and aerobic in nature.

WORKOUT B - 45 MINUTE EXAMPLE

Warm-Up
Activation Exercises
Workout:

Total workout time 45 minutes.

A1 15 kcal Assault Bike at 2 Min Pace
A2 25% Max Push-Ups x 5 reps (20 Max Test)
A3 15Kcal Assault Bike at 2 Min Pace
A4 25% Max TRX/Ring Rows x 7 reps (28 Max Test)

Repeat. No Rest.

You should feel at the end of the workout that you could continue going for another 60 minutes.

Stretch

Workout C

Warm-Up
Activation Exercises
Workout:

Total workout time 20 minutes.

A1 250m Row at Pace
A2 Pull Ups at 25% Max
A3 Goblet Squats (Medium) x 10
A4 Single Arm Kettlebell Carry at 30 Seconds Per Arm

No Rest. Repeat.

*Each 250m row must be EXACTLY THE SAME split time.

**Maintain steady pace throughout. All four exercises should take exactly the same time each set.

If you cannot maintain pace, slow down and reduce pace for next time.

You should feel at the end of the workout that you could continue going for another 60 minutes.

Stretch

Workout C - Notes

250m Rowing Pace

Row with your feet out the straps. This is for efficiency of transfer from one exercise to another and a skill-based drill to improve your rowing leg drive. Choose a pace that is sustainable and repeatable in nature. This means **each 250m row time must be identical**. Your pace shouldn't fluctuate. If you can't hit the same pace for each set, you haven't earned the right to progress. This is a skill in itself.

For example, a correct set should read 1:05, 1:05, 1:05, etc.

If it reads 1:02, 1:17, 1:09, etc., this is not correct, and you need to spend time practicing the skill of repeated set. The pace you choose should be easy in nature. At the end of the workout, you should feel that you could continue going for another 60 minutes.

If not, slow down next time.

Not sure what time to start with, our suggestion:

Men: 1:08 | Women: 1:15

Adjust accordingly up or down until all working sets are identical in nature.

25% Max Pull-Ups

Prior to starting this work out, ideally a separate day when you are not fatigued, perform a max pull-up test (over hand grip).

Each pull-up should be performed at a 31x1 tempo (3 seconds down, 1 second pause, explode up, 1 second pause). Good pull-up technique is recommended.

During the workout, you'll only be performing 25% of your max effort. That's a 1:4 ratio.

Working example:

Pull-Up Test = 3 reps

Rep scheme during Workout B = 1 rep

Goblet Squats

Choose a light to medium weight that you can swing comfortably to perform 20 reps.

Each goblet squat should be performed at a 31x1 tempo (3 seconds down, 1 second pause, explode up, 1 second pause).

Weight suggestions:
Men: 16kg-32kg kettlebell
Women: 8kg-20kg kettlebell

Single Arm Kettlebell Carry

Choose a light to medium weight that you can swing comfortably and carry in one arm. As you carry it, ensure your pinky finger is almost touching your leg, palm facing forward. Shoulders back and down. Carry in one arm for 30 seconds, and then switch arms. You need to go lighter than you think. As we progress, grip over a period of 45 minutes is essential and make sure you don't overuse it for the pull-ups and row. Think of this as an abdominal exercise.

Weight suggestions:
Men: 12kg-32kg kettlebell
Women: 8kg-20kg kettlebell

The Progression

Once you can complete 20 minutes comfortably, you simply increase the time by 5 minutes each workout, up to a total of 45 minutes.

It could look like this:
Week 1: 20 Minutes
Week 2: 25 Minutes
Week 3: 30 Minutes
Week 4: 35 Minutes
Week 5: 40 Minutes
Week 6: 45 Minutes

However, the rules when you increase are as follows:

1. Your row time remains exactly the same. For example, if you rowed in 1:10 each set during the first 20 minutes, you continue rowing at 1:10. You do not increase or decrease the pace.

2. You must complete all sets and reps of pull-ups and goblet squats.

3. Each working set must be identical in time, you're not gasping for breath, and you're taking your time between exercises.

The final 45-minute workout could look like this:

WORKOUT C - 45 MINUTE EXAMPLE

Warm-Up
Activation Exercises
Workout:

C1 **250m Row at 1:10**
C2 **Pull Ups x 4 Reps (16 Rep Max)**
C3 **Goblet Squats x 10 x 20kg**
C4 **Single Arm Kettlebell Carry x 16kg,**
     30 Seconds Per Arm

No Rest. Repeat.

*Each 250m row must be EXACTLY THE SAME split time.

**Maintain steady pace throughout. All four exercises should take exactly the same time each set. If you cannot maintain pace, slow down and reduce pace for next time.

You should feel at the end of the workout that you could continue going for another 60 minutes.

Stretch

Walk/Run - WR

Warm-Up
Workout:

Total time 30 minutes.

Option A - Walk 30 Min at MAF

Option B - Walk/Run 30 Min (Run 1 min, Walk 4 min) at MAF

Option C - Run 30 Min at MAF (180 - Age)

At the end of 30 minutes, you should feel like you could keep going for another 2 hours. This is easy, aerobic work.

Stretch

Walk/Run - Notes

Aerobic Base Building

At Strength Matters, we prioritize the aerobic energy system above all other systems. Human beings are designed to be aerobic. The more aerobic we are, the more resilient we can be in life. Therefore, we ask that you do not underestimate the importance of the Walk/Run prescription during your proven training plan.

Aerobic endurance training cannot be forgotten and is the single greatest contribution a coach can add to an athlete's program. This is all about working below your Aerobic Threshold so that we can help speed recovery between higher-intensity workouts later in the program while building your aerobic base.

Option A,B, or C: You Choose

We have provided three options for you here, which depend entirely on:

- **Your experience and ability to run**

- **How your body is feeling on any particular day**

If you are new to running, we recommend going with Option A in week 1, then potentially progressing to Option B in week 2 or 3. For the advanced and more experienced runner, Option 3 might be the best option. Either way, listen to your body and choose an option that best fits how you feel on that particular day.

Understanding MAF - Maximum Aerobic Function

This is our preferred method of calculating your aerobic threshold. It ensures that we stay in the aerobic zone and work on building your aerobic speed. When we say at MAF in the training plan, we ask that you keep your heart rate below a certain level at all times. As a general rule, your MAF HR is 180 minus your age.

For example, if you are 40 and in good health, then your MAF heart rate will be:

180 - 40 = 140.

The Progression

The progression of this workout is volume based. Once you can complete 30 minutes comfortably, you simply increase the time by 15 minutes each week, up until a total of 60 minutes.

It could look like this:
Week 1: 30 Minutes
Week 2: 30 Minutes
Week 3: 45 Minutes
Week 4: 45 Minutes
Week 5: 60 Minutes
Week 6: 60 Minutes

The rules when you increase are as follows:

1. You must feel refreshed and energized at the end of each workout.

2. You never exceed your MAF heart rate or go lower than 10 beats less than MAF

The final 60-minute workout could look like this:

WORKOUT C - 45 MINUTE EXAMPLE

Warm-Up

Workout:

Total time 60 minutes.

Athlete Age: 40

Option A - Walk 60 Min at MAF 140 HR

Option B - Walk/Run 60 Min (Run 1 min, Walk 4 min) at MAF 140 HR

Option C - Run 60 Min at MAF 140 HR

At the end of 60 minutes, you should feel like you could keep going for another 3 hours. This is easy, aerobic work.

Stretch

Hike - H

Warm-Up

Workout:

Total time: Minimum - 60 minutes.
Maximum - 4 Hours.

Get outside in the fresh air. Find a hill or mountain, the steeper the better, and build some good miles into your legs.

*For advanced athletes, wear a weight vest 10-40lbs.

Stretch

Hike - Notes

The benefits of hiking go far beyond working out, even though we are building miles into your legs. A good walk outside or a regular hike can have a huge impact on our mental health, allowing us to switch off from stressful thoughts and think more rationally, all while being at one with nature.

We're big fans of hiking at Strength Matters as it can:

1. **Clear your mind**

2. **Boost your brain and restore cognitive functions**

3. **Improve your outlook on life**

4. **Get you to unplug from the digital world**

Get outside, get some Vitamin D, and enjoy nature. You'll be surprised how it will impact your training over the course of this training plan.

Phase 2:
Rev the Engine

Rev the Engine Training

Build on the foundation.

Duration: 6-18 weeks.

Rev the Engine Schedule

Your training will consist of six days a week training and will include one rest day. Workouts will last no more than 60 minutes, and some will be as short as 25 minutes. Depending on your training and skill levels, this program should last between 6-18 weeks, at the earliest 6 weeks if you can accomplish the required goals.

The volume and intensity will increase on workout E and the track days. Workout E should feel easy throughout, whereas the track days will be more fatiguing. This is more aerobic power. If it feels easy to begin with, don't push it. Again, we're working in conjunction with the central nervous system here. It will soon get hard, trust me, when we approach phase 3.

Choose your weights accordingly. Only you can decide what is right for you and your body. From experience, it's better to err on the lighter side than to drop down in weight mid-set. You will need to go lighter than you think.

Mon	Tue	Wed	Thurs	Fri	Sat	Sun
D	TD	WR	E	TD	Rest	H

As you can see the schedule consists of a D + Track Day & E + Track Day split with two Walk/Run sessions and one complete day of rest. The workouts will remain the same. The intensity and volume will change with each workout. Your body will dictate what you do on the Walk/Run days. The WR days are meant to be easy in nature, and only you can decide the intensity at which you perform them. Volume here is more important than the intensity.

Equipment

For this phase of training, you will require the following equipment:

4. **Barbell + Plates**

5. **Kettlebells (in pairs)**

6. **Concept 2 Rowing Machine (or equivalent)**

7. **Athletic Track**

8. **Running Shoes**

Warm Up: 5-10 Minutes

Prior to all training sessions, we recommend completing a thorough warm-up alongside purposeful activation exercises. You need to take the time to mobilize thoroughly. Never underestimate the power of a good warm-up and the importance it plays going into your workout. This is a required element of this training plan. All workouts must begin with a thorough warm-up and activation work.

Activation Work: 5-10 Minutes

The Phase 2 activation circuit differs from Phase 1, but to keep things simple you will perform the following warm-up and activation series prior to each workout in phase 2.

Perform 3 rounds. No rest. Perform only one round. 60 seconds for each exercise.

A1 Cobra Pose to Downward Dog.

A2 Dragon Pumps. (30 seconds each side)

A3 Hand Bridge and reach. Alternate sides.

A4 Bird Dogs.

A5 Same Side Bird Dogs.

A6 Side Plank Rotations. (30 Seconds Each Side)

A7 Dead Bugs

A8 Leopard Crawl - 10 Steps Forwards/10 Steps Backwards.

Stretch: 2-10 Minutes

We believe that all everyday athletes should stretch for 5-10 minutes at the end of every training session (unless in a rare circumstance such as hyper-mobility). Post-workout stretching, while the soft tissue is warm and malleable and will offer faster improvements.

We have three basic stretching principles:

1. **Diaphragmatic breathing is fundamental to increasing range of motion.**

2. **Contract-relax stretching trumps static stretching.**

3. **Any stretch should take a minimum of 2 minutes.**

We understand that most people skip this portion of the workout; however, do so at your peril. If you are lacking time, we recommend focusing on one area and doing that one area well!

Phase 2 is running centric. You need to spend a lot of time on the hamstrings, hips, calves and piriformis. Here is a list of stretching exercises we would highly recommend performing regularly during Phase 2:

- **Lying hamstring stretch with band**

- **Couch/Tree Stretch**

- **Hip flexor stretches**

- **Butterfly Stretch**

- **Seated Spinal Twist**

- **Frog Stretch**

- **Piriformis Stretch**

- **Curb stretch (for calves)**

- **Pigeon Stretch**

Workout D

Warm-Up
Activation Exercises
Workout:

Part 1: Strength Circuit
Total workout time 20 minutes.
AMRAP (As Many Rounds As Possible)

A1 Barbell Suitcase Deadlift x 8/8
A2 Offset Double Kettlebell Front Squats x 8
A3 Barbell Bent Over Row x 8
A4 Offset Double Kettlebell Military press x 8/8

8 Reps must be completed on each round.
If you struggle half-way through, you've gone too heavy. Reduce weight next time.

Part 2: Recovery Row
Row 500m at set pace.
Rest 1 Minute. Repeat x 3.
Set the rower for 500m intervals with 1-minute rest. All 500m should be identical in time! For example, 2:10, 2:10, 2:10, and you should feel like you could continue for a further 60 minutes.

Stretch

Workout D - Notes

Barbell Suitcase Deadlift

This is one of the most humbling strength exercises that you will perform in this program. If you haven't done this before, it challenges your grip, abs, and glutes simultaneously, and will highlight any weakness you have. It provides a significant neurological overload to the body.

Using a barbell can be tricky when first starting out because of the balance required. Stick with it, it will come, and you will get better at doing it.

Choose a weight that you can comfortably do 8 reps with multiple times over the course of 20 minutes on your weaker side. You will need to go lighter than you think to begin with, but your body will adapt quickly. If you do not have a barbell, a kettlebell is a great alternative but will not provide the desired effect.

Weight Starting Suggestions:
Men: Olympic Bar + 2 x 10kg Plates
Women: Olympic Bar + 2 x 2.5kg Plates

Double Offset Kettlebell Front Squats and Military Press

Choose two kettlebells that have at least 4kg and no more than 8kg difference between them. For example, 24kg + 16kg or 12kg + 8kg.

Incorporating offset loading into your training is a great way to increase core and hip stability, and correct any imbalances you may have. It enhances strength development by improving stability and eradicating any weak links in the body. This will light up your core, and it is not uncommon for you to feel extremely hungry post workout, be warned.

Choose weights with which so you can comfortably complete all 8 reps on both sides for the full twenty minutes. With offset work, make sure you switch sides every set so you work both sides equally. For example, if you start with the lighter weight on your left side, make sure you complete the next set on your right side with the lighter weight.

Barbell Bent Over Row

Choose a light to medium weight that you can comfortably perform 8 reps. Each bent over row should be performed at a 31x1 tempo (3 seconds down, 1 second pause, explode up, 1 second pause).

If you do not have access to a barbell, potential alternatives are:

1. **TRX/Ring Row Pull**
2. **Kettlebell Renegade Row (both sides)**

Recovery Row

Row with your feet out of the straps. This is a skill-based drill to improve your rowing leg drive. Choose a pace that is sustainable and repeatable. This means each 500m row time must be identical. Your pace shouldn't fluctuate. If you can't hit the same pace for each set, you haven't earned the right to progress. This is a skill in and of itself.

For example, a correct set should read 2:12, 2:12, 2:12, etc.

If it reads 2:02, 1:57, 2:12, etc., you need to spend time practicing the skill of repeated set. The pace you choose should be easy. At the end of the workout, you should feel that you could continue for another 60 minutes. If not, slow down next time.

Not sure what pace to start with, our suggestion:

Men: 2:16
Women: 2:26

Adjust accordingly up or down until all working sets are identical and the pace best suites for your needs.

Strength Circuit Progression

The progression of the strength circuit is a density model. Each week, you are trying to perform more working sets in the given time frame. Once you feel you have reached the maximum number of rounds you can perform, then you can look to increase the weights on the exercises given. In theory, by the end, you should be able to perform this routine with virtually no rest. Only then, do you look to increase the weights and increase your resting time between sets.

The progression could look like this:
Week 1: 4 Rounds
Week 2: 5 Rounds
Week 3: 6 Rounds
Week 4: 6 Rounds
Week 5: 4 Rounds (Increased weights)
Week 6: 4 Rounds (Same weights as previous week)

Recovery Row Progression

Your first week will start with three sets. Every week you are going to progress the number of working sets by 1 up to a maximum of 8. However, before you progress from three in the first week, you must ensure that all working sets are the same and you develop your skill levels in producing repeatable and consistent times. Your pace shouldn't fluctuate from week to week. It needs to be consistent. You will only increase your pace once you can do all 8 sets.

Workout E

Warm-Up

Activation Exercises

Workout:

Row | Clean | Row | Press | Repeat

Total Time: 20 minutes work.

A1 **Row 250m at Pace**

A2 **Double Offset KB Clean x 15**

A3 **Row 250m at Pace**

A4 **Double Offset KB Military Press**
     (No Re-Cleaning) x 15

Repeat for the 20 minutes.

This is sustained, aerobic type work.
Don't try and kill yourself.

Tip: Set the concept 2 rower to 250m intervals
and 1-minute rest.

Stretch

Workout E - Notes

250m Rowing Pace:

Row with your feet out the straps. This is for
efficiency of transfer from one exercise to another
and a skill-based drill to improve your rowing
leg drive. Choose a pace that is sustainable and
repeatable in nature. This means **each 250m row time
must be identical**. Your pace shouldn't fluctuate. If
you can't hit the same pace for each set, you haven't
earned the right to progress. This is a skill in itself.

For example, a correct set should read 1:08, 1:08,
2:08, etc. If it reads 1:02, 1:17, 1:12, etc., this is not
correct, and you need to spend time practicing the
skill of repeated set. The pace you choose should be
easy in nature. At the end of the workout, you should
feel that you could continue going for another 60
minutes. If not, slow down next time.

Not sure what time to start with, our suggestion:

Men: 1:08

Women: 1:16

Adjust accordingly up or down until all working sets
are identical in nature.

Tip: Set the concept 2 rower to 250m intervals and
1-minute rest.

Double Offset Kettlebell Front Squats and Military Press

Choose two kettlebells that have at least 4kg and no more than 8kg difference between them. For example, 24kg + 16kg or 12kg + 8kg.

Incorporating offset loading into our training is a great way to increase core and hip stability, and correct any imbalances we may have. It enhances further strength development by improving stability and eradicating any weak links in the body. This will light up your core significantly, and it is not too uncommon for you to feel extremely hungry post workout. So be warned. With offset work, make sure you switch sides every set, so you work both sides equally. For example, if you start with the lighter weight on your left side, make sure you complete the next set on your right side with the lighter weight.

Tip: Choose a weight that you can complete 20 reps of military press, on both sides.

Working example:

Men: 20kg max press for 20 reps. Weight for cleans and military press = 20kg + 12kg.

Women: 12kg max press for 20 reps. Weight for cleans and military press = 12kg + 8kg.

Row | Clean | Row | Press | Repeat - Progression

The progression of this workout is simple. I didn't say easy. I said simple. Once you can complete 20 minutes comfortably and can complete ALL 15 reps with presses and cleans, you simply increase the time by 5 minutes each workout, up to a total of 45 minutes.

It could look like this:
Week 1: 20 Minutes
Week 2: 25 Minutes
Week 3: 30 Minutes
Week 4: 35 Minutes
Week 5: 40 Minutes
Week 6: 45 Minutes

However, the rules when you increase are as follows:

- Your row time remains exactly the same. For example, if you rowed in 1:08 each set during the first 20-minutes, you continue rowing at 1:08. You do not increase or decrease the pace.

- You must complete all sets and reps of kettlebell cleans and presses.

- The 1:00 rest period remains a constant.

The final 45-minute workout could look like this:

WORKOUT E - 45-MINUTE EXAMPLE

Warm-Up
Activation Exercises
Workout:

Row | Clean | Row | Press | Repeat
Total time: 45 minutes.

A1 Row 250m at 1:08 Pace
A2 Double Offset KB Clean (20kg + 12kg) x 15
A3 Row 250m at 1:08 Pace
A4 Double Offset KB Military Press
　　(20kg + 12kg) x 15
Repeat for the 45 minutes.

This is sustained, aerobic type work. Don't try and kill yourself.

Tip: Set the Concept 2 rower to 250m intervals and 1-minute rest.

Stretch

Track/Day - TD

Warm-Up

Workout:

Total workout time 40-60 minutes

Part 1: Run 1 Mile Easy at MAF HR
Rest 2-5 Minutes
Part 2: 400m x 3 at 80% effort. Rest 2 Minutes
Between Sets.
Rest 7 Minutes
Part 3: 400m x 3 at 80% effort. Rest 2 Minutes
Between Sets.

All 400m times must be virtually identical. Never
more than your 80% calculated time and never
faster than 3 seconds.

At the end of the session, you should feel like you
have worked out, yet still feel energized. This is
aerobic power work.

Stretch

Time in seconds = 90 Seconds

90 x 1.2 = 108 seconds

108 - 90 = 18 seconds

80% effort time = 1 minute 20 seconds

+ 18 seconds = 1 minute 38 seconds.

Track Day - Notes

400m Max Effort Testing

Prior to starting this phase, we highly recommend
testing your 400m max effort time to calculate your
80% pace effort.

To do this we recommend the following:

Warm-Up

Workout:

Part 1: Run 1 Mile, Easy at MAF HR
Rest 2-5 Minutes
Part 2: 400m Max Effort
Active Recovery
Part 3 (Optional): Run 1 Mile, Easy at MAF HR

Once you have your time, calculate your 80% time.

Working Example:

400m Max Effort = 1 minute 20 seconds

400m Aerobic Power Repeats

We are progressing from aerobic threshold training to
aerobic power training in this phase. This isn't to be
confused with anaerobic training. This type of training
should never be trained to exhaustion. This should feel
like a moderately difficult pace, yet repeatable and
sustainable in nature.

The key to this is that you can **complete ALL 400m
repeats in the same time frame**. (There is some leeway
to go faster than the prescribed time but no more than
3 seconds.) If you cannot complete all 400m in the
same time frame in the first week, 80% is too much for
you, and you should drop down to 70% and try again.

Track Alternatives

Not everyone has access to an athletic track. If that is
the case, you will switch out the 400m track repeats
with ¼ mile repeats, using your smart watch as a guide.
Find somewhere that you can train outdoors It needs to
be relatively flat and doesn't require you to stop in that
¼ mile. Complete the workout exactly as above.

Walk/Run - WR

Warm-Up

Workout:

Total time 60 minutes.

Option A - Walk/Run 60 Min (Run 2 min, Walk 3 min) at MAF

Option B - Run 60 Min at MAF (180 - Age)

At the end of 60 minutes, you should feel like you could keep going for another 3 hours. This is easy aerobic work.

Stretch

Walk/Run - Notes

Aerobic Base Building Continued:

We ask that you do not underestimate the importance of the Walk/Run prescription. This is all about maintaining the aerobic treshold work you put in during Phase 1 so that you can recover faster during the higher-intensity workouts in Phase 3.

Option A or B: You Choose

We have provided two options for you here, which depend entirely on:

- **Your experience and ability to run**
- **How your body is feeling on this particular day**

If you are relatively new to running having completed phase 1, we recommend going with Option A in week 1, then potentially progressing to Option B in week 4 or 5. For the advanced and more experienced runner, Option 2 might be the best option. Either way, listen to your body and choose an option that best fits how you feel on that particular day.

Understanding MAF - Maximum Aerobic Function

This is Strength Matters preferred method of calculating your aerobic threshold. It ensures that we stay in the aerobic zone and work on building your aerobic speed. When we say at MAF in the training plan, we ask that you keep your heart rate below a certain level at all times. As a general rule, your MAF HR is 180 minus your age.

For example 40 and in good health, then your MAF heart rate will be:

180 - 40 = 140.

For Option B Athletes Only:

If you decide to run the entire time at MAF, you will need to train in your MAF training zone. This means you have to keep your heart rate no lower than 10 beats per your MAF and never over.

Working Example:

Age = 40

MAF = 180 - 40 = 140

HR Training Range = 130 - 140 at all times.

Progression

Over the weeks, you'll want to monitor the distance covered and speed at which you perform, all while keeping your heart rate below MAF. This is the key. Please don't stray above your MAF Heart Rate. If you feel tired on a given day, choose the easier option. It's not about going guns blazing. It's about leaving you fresh for the next session.

The rules are similar to Phase 1:

- **You must feel refreshed and energized at the end of each workout**
- **You never exceed your MAF heart rate**

It is completely tailored to my needs and goals. I have not been disappointed.

Andrew Ellis, Everyday Athlete.

A transformative approach to personal training that finally solves the problem of the other 160+ hours in the week. An unprecedented leap in how personal training is delivered and a mind-blowing experience to match. Visit **www.strengthmatters.com** today to start your personal coaching experience.

STRENGTH MATTERS®

MADE FOR **LIFE**

Phase 3: Refine the Engine

Refine the Engine Training

Build the anaerobic engine. Start to peak. Duration: Maximum 6 weeks.

Goals

1. Progress to 60 minutes of Get Up Master and Crawl Master workouts.

2. See significant progress in Rowing Gainzzz and Hill Sprints.

3. Avoid burn out and exhaustion.

Refine the Engine Schedule

Your schedule will consist of five days a week training and will include two active rest days, back to back. Workouts will last no more than 60 minutes, and some will be as short as 30 minutes. This part of the program should last **no longer than 6 weeks**. Anything more than 6 weeks and you will start to fatigue and burn out. This is about developing the anaerobic system, and it's not designed to be sustainable in nature.

The volume will increase on Get Up Master and Crawl Master. This is all about developing work capacity. Meanwhile Rowing Gainzzz, The Lactate Bath, and Hill Sprints are all about working to maximum intensity. The volume AND intensity will increase as you progress. It is not for the faint hearted. We're working in conjunction with the central nervous system here. Everything you have done up to this point has been building to this. However, we can't overdo it in this phase, or we'll undo all the great work you've accomplished so far.

Similarly, you can't expect to jump into this phase right away. You need to build the base from Phase 1 and Phase 2. I would even recommend a recovery week of doing NOTHING prior to starting this after completing Phase 2. You need to choose your weights accordingly. Only you can decide what is right for you and your body. From experience, it's better to err on the lighter side than dropping down in weight mid-set. You will need to go lighter than you think.

Mon	Tue	Wed	Thurs	Fri	Sat	Sun
GUM	RG	CM	LB	WR	Hike	HS

As you can see, the schedule consists of an aerobic capacity workout + anaerobic workout schedule in a 2:3 ratio. It also includes two recovery Walk/Run and hiking sessions back to back for recovery purposes. The workouts will remain the same. The intensity and volume will change with each workout. Your body will dictate what you do on the Walk/Run and hike days. The Walk/Run and hike days are meant to be easy and only you can decide the intensity at which you perform them. Volume here is more important than intensity. Do not skip these days.

Equipment

For this phase of training, you will require the following pieces of equipment:

4. **Barbell + Plates**

5. **Kettlebells (Pairs)**

6. **Concept 2 Rowing Machine (or equivalent)**

7. **Running Shoes**

Warm Up: 5-10 Minutes

Prior to all training sessions, we recommend completing a thorough warm-up alongside purposeful activation exercises. You need to take the time to mobilize thoroughly. Never underestimate the power of a good warm-up and the importance it plays going into your workout. This is a non-negotiable element of this training plan. All workouts must begin with a thorough warm-up and activation work.

The phase 3 activation circuit differs from phase 1 and 2, but to keep things simple, you will perform the following warm-up and activation series prior to each workout in phase 3.

Activation Work: 5-10 Minutes

Perform only one round. 60 seconds for each exercise.

A1 Diaphragmatic Breathing: Prone

A2 Six Point Rocking

A3 Six Point Neck Nods

A4 Bird Dogs

A5 Same Side Bird Dogs

A6 McGill Curl Up

A7 Deep Squat Sit + Hip Pry

A8 Standing Ankle Invert/Evert Drill

Stretch: 2-10 Minutes

We understand that most people skip this portion of the workout; however, do so at your peril. If you are lacking time, we recommend focusing on one area, and doing that one area well! Phase 3 is again very much running and rowing centric. You need to spend a lot of time on the hamstrings, hips, calves, and piriformis.

Here is a list of stretching exercises we would highly recommend performing regularly during phase 3:

- **Lying hamstring stretch with band**

- **Couch/Tree Stretch**

- **Hip flexor stretches**

- **Butterfly Stretch**

- **Hurdler Stretch**

- **Frog Stretch**

- **Piriformis Stretch**

- **Curb stretch (for calves)**

- **Pigeon Stretch**

- **Bretzel Stretch**

Workout - GUM

Warm-Up

Activation Exercises

Workout:

Total workout time 30 minutes.

A1 Row 500m at Easy Pace

A1 Turkish Get Up x 1/1 at Light Weight within 1 Minute

Repeat.

Continuous work. No rest between exercises.

**This is about work capacity.

**Each 500m Row time MUST be identical.

Set rower to 500m intervals with 1 min rest.
If you can't complete get ups in 1 min, adjust weight accordingly.

Stretch

Get Up Master (GUM) - Notes

500m Rowing Pace

Row with your feet out of the straps. This is for efficiency of transfer from one exercise to another and a skill based drill to improve your rowing leg drive. Choose a pace that is sustainable and repeatable in nature. This means each 500m row time must be identical. Your pace shouldn't fluctuate. If you can't hit the same pace for each set, you haven't earned the right to progress. This is a skill in itself. For example, a correct set should read 2:12, 2:12, 2:12, etc. If it reads 2:02, 1:57, 2:12, etc., this is not correct, and you need to spend time practicing the skill of repeated set. The pace you choose should be easy in nature. At the end of the workout, you should feel that you could continue going for another 60 minutes. If not, slow down next time.

Not sure what time to start with, our suggestion:

Men: 2:16
Women: 2:26

Adjust accordingly up or down until all working sets are identical.

Turkish Get Up (TGU)

Choose a weight that is 50% of your maximum effort. Combined with the volume of rowing, you will need to **go lighter** than you think. Only once you can complete the full prescription of 60 minutes can you then increase the weight in this workout. It's important to balance technique and speed with this workout. Each get up should take approximately 25 seconds for you to complete. This gives a 10-second window of transitioning on and off the rower.

Get Up Master Workout Progression

The progression of this workout is time based over a period of six weeks. Once you can complete 30 minutes comfortably, you simply increase the time by 15 minutes every two weeks, up to a total of 60 minutes.

It will look like this:
Week 1: 30 Minutes
Week 2: 30 Minutes
Week 3: 45 Minutes
Week 4: 45 Minutes
Week 5: 60 Minutes
Week 6: 60 Minutes

However, the rules when you increase are as follows:

1. Your row time remains exactly the same. For example, if you rowed in 1:08 each set during the first 30 minutes, you continue rowing at 1:08. You do not increase or decrease the pace.

2. You must complete all the reps of Turkish get ups in the given time frame.

The final 60-minute workout could look like this:

WORKOUT GUM - 60 MINUTE EXAMPLE

Warm-Up
Activation Exercises

Workout:
Total time 30 minutes.

A1 Row 500m at 1:12 Pace
A2 Turkish Get Up 1/1 at 16kg within 1 Minute

Repeat

Continuous work. No rest between exercises.

**This is about work capacity.
**Each 500m Row time MUST be identical.

Set rower to 500m intervals with 1 min rest.
If you can't complete get ups in 1 min, adjust weight accordingly.

Stretch

Workout: Crawl Master (CM)

Warm-Up
Activation Exercises

Workout:

Total time: 30 minutes.

A1 Run 1/4 Mile or 400m at MAF
A2 Box Crawl. 4 laps around an object.
Repeat.

Repeat for 30 minutes.

Continuous work. No rest between exercises.

**HR Must stay below MAF at all times DURING THE RUN. This is about building aerobic speed and work capacity.

**Change your running speed accordingly to fit the HR

Stretch

Workout CM - Notes

Running

You can choose to do this either indoors on a treadmill or outdoors, whatever is most convenient for you. The key to this workout is making sure you **run the entire time at your MAF pace**, outlined below.

Running Pace & Understanding MAF - Maximum Aerobic Function

This is our preferred method of calculating your aerobic threshold. It ensures that we stay in the aerobic zone and work on building your aerobic speed. When we say at MAF in the training plan, we ask that you keep your heart rate below a certain level at all times. As a general rule, your MAF HR is 180 minus your age. So, if for example you are 40 and in good health, then your MAF heart rate will be:

180 - 40 = 140.

Working Example:

Age = 40
MAF = 180 - 40 = 140

HR Training Range = 130 - 140 at all times.

Running Alternatives

Some days it may not be possible to run, or past injuries may not make this possible. Don't worry. We have alternate solutions. Simply choose from one of the three following pieces of equipment and switch running for one of these:

- **Assault Bike**
- **Concept 2 Rower**
- **Ski Erg**

Crawl Master Workout Progression

The progression of this workout is time based over a period of six weeks. Once you can complete 30 minutes comfortably, you simply increase the time by 15 minutes every two weeks, up to a total of 60-minutes.

It will look like this:
Week 1: 30 Minutes
Week 2: 30 Minutes
Week 3: 45 Minutes
Week 4: 45 Minutes
Week 5: 60 Minutes
Week 6: 60 Minutes

Workout: Rowing Gainzzz (RG)

Warm-Up

Specific Activation Work:
Three rounds. No rest.

A1 Single Leg Kettlebell Deadlift x 5/5
A2 Overhead Kettlebell Squat x 5/5
A3 Dumbbell Side Plank Rotations x 5/5
    Row 500m at Easy Pace

Workout:

Part 1: Appetizer
Total Time: 15 Min

15 Min Circuit.

A1 Single Leg Barbell RDL x 5/5
A2 One Arm One Leg Row x 5/5
A3 Offset Barbell Lunges x 5/5
A4 Single Arm Kettlebell Carry 30 sec / 30 sec

Repeat. Continuous Work. No Rest.

Use light to medium weights.
This is the appetizer for the main event.

Part 2: Alactic Rowing Gainzzz
Row X number of calories in 20 seconds.
Rest 2 minutes.

Repeat until you can no longer hit X number of
calories or have completed 10 rounds.

Tip: Set rower to X number of calories and 2-minute
rest intervals.

Stretch

Workout RG - Notes

Testing Prior to This Workout

Prior to this workout you will need to test the following:

·   Max Calories in 20 seconds on a concept 2 rower.

·   You can have three attempts with as much rest
    as you need in between. What you're looking
    for is your best score.

For example:
Effort One = 9 Kcal
Effort Two = 10 Kcal
Effort Three = 10 Kcal

Your best score here would be 10 Kcal, and that is your
goal for each 20 second interval.

Activation

For this particular workout, we have prescribed specific
activation work to prepare you for the main workout.
Please follow as prescribed and use lighter weights
than normal to complete.

Part 1: Appetizer

This workout should be a light to moderate effort.
The goal is not to fully exert yourself here. The main
event, **rowing, is the most important part of this
workout**. Make sure you are refreshed enough to
complete that workout.

Single Leg Barbell Romanian Deadlift

The important thing with this exercise is control. It's
not about how much weight you can lift, but how well
you can do it. This is all about hinge patterning, and
this exercise has a huge role in improving hip and spine
mechanics during most movements and enhancing
injury resilience.

Weight suggestions:
Men and Women: 70% Max Effort

One Arm One Leg Row

This is quite possibly one of my favorite exercises for core stability and anti-rotational work. For years, I looked at the single arm dumbbell bench press and thought, What's the antithesis of that? Well, this is what I came up with.

Grab a pair of medium to light dumbbells or kettlebells. Err on the side of caution with the weight the first time you try the renegade row. You'll probably need weights with a flat side to rest on. Round dumbbells may roll under the inexperienced. Get into a press-up position with a dumbbell/kettlebell in each hand. Brace your body, then raise one of the dumbbells, and then raise the opposite leg, supporting yourself on the other arm and other leg. The movement is once again more important than the weight being lifted.

Offset Barbell Lunges

Think movement not load. This is designed specifically to challenge core stability in a locomotive lunge pattern. You will need to practice this movement prior to doing this exercise to find the optimal weight. Go lighter to begin with so it doesn't throw you all over the place.

Load a barbell in the racked position on one side only. For example, 10kg on one side. You are going to unrack the bar, stepping forwards and not backwards. This is the opposite of what you would normally do. Complete the set of lunges and re-rack the bar. You will notice the barbell is now the opposite way round to how you

started. This method ensures you work both sides evenly without having to think about barbell positions.

Single Arm Kettlebell Carry

Choose a medium weight that you can comfortably carry in one arm. As you carry it, ensure your pinky finger is almost touching your leg, palm facing forward. Shoulders back and down. Carry in one arm for 30 seconds, then switch arms. You need to go lighter than you think. As we progress, the rowing is the most important component of the workout, and grip over a period of 45 minutes is essential. Make sure you don't overdo it. Think of this as an abdominal exercise.

Weight suggestions:
Men: 12kg-32kg kettlebell
Women: 8kg-20kg kettlebell

Part 2: Alactic Rowing Gainzzz

This is the main event. You will be giving a 110% effort and leaving everything on the playing field. This is not for the faint hearted. But at the same time you need to be controlled and measured in what you do. There are certain rules you have to follow to get maximum benefits and also ensure you stay fresh enough to complete all the other workouts during the week.

The Alactic Rowing Gainzzz Workout

I can't emphasize the importance of sticking to the rules in this workout. This is not about making yourself sick OR trying to complete all ten sets every single week.

The goal is to complete ten sets of X number of calories within 2 minutes. Perfectly. What I mean by perfectly is that all your sets are identical in nature. So that means, if your score was 10 Kcal in testing, ten sets of 10Kcal with 2 min rest between must be completed.

If you produce results like this...
Set 1: 10 Kcal in 20 seconds
Set 2: 10 Kcal in 20 seconds
Set 3: 10 Kcal in 20 seconds
Set 4: 10 Kcal in 20 seconds
Set 5: 9 Kcal in 20 seconds
... you are done for the day.

We are flirting with your alactic anaerobic threshold, not trying to exceed it and fatigue the central nervous system. You must stop to give your body ample time to rest and recuperate for the other workouts. If you don't stick to this protocol, it will have a detrimental effect on your results.

On the flip side, if you produce perfect results of 10 perfect sets the first time up, I would suggest re-testing your max 20 second calorie test. This is all about going to the point of failure. At seconds 21 and 22, you should be done and out for the count. You should not feel like you can go again immediately.

If it is still the same, continue the progression (outlined below), then later drop back down to the 20-second protocol. This may be the kick-starter your alactic anaerobic system needs to allow you to go deep enough into your central nervous system.

Rowing Gainzzz Progression

The progression of this workout is based primarily on the rowing section. In Part 1, you can adjust the weights accordingly; however, you should always feel refreshed and ready to attack the rowing section. Use it as a primer for rowing. If you feel fatigued going into the rowing section, you have got this wrong.

Once you can complete ten sets of 20-second intervals perfectly (all calories the same), you will re-start the process, except you are increasing the time to 25 seconds. This means re-testing your 25-second calorie marker and starting again. You will follow this process, adding 5 seconds up to a maximum of 40 seconds.

It goes:
1.   **20 Second Interval Calories + 2 Min Rest**
2.   **25 Second Interval Calories + 2:30 Min Rest**
3.   **30 Second Interval Calories + 3 Min Rest**
4.   **35 Second Interval Calories + 3:30 Min Rest**
5.   **40 Second Interval Calories + 4 Min Rest**

It is highly unlikely you will reach 40 seconds in 6 weeks. If you do, the protocol hasn't been completed effectively and/or you are not strong enough to go deep enough into your alactic anaerobic system. If you

can complete ten sets of 20 second intervals perfectly, followed by 25 seconds the next week and then 30 seconds the week after, you need to drop back down to 20 seconds and re-test to follow the protocol. In theory, this should not be possible, but sometimes can happen when the body has not yet adapted to this type of anaerobic treshold training.

25 Second Working Example:

25 Second Test:
Effort One = 13 Kcal
Effort Two = 14 Kcal
Effort Three = 11 Kcal

Your best score here would be 14 Kcal, and that is your goal for each 25 second interval.

Example: first effort workout at 25 second intervals:
Set 1: 14 Kcal in 25 seconds
Set 2: 14 Kcal in 25 seconds
Set 3: 14 Kcal in 25 seconds
Set 4: 14 Kcal in 25 seconds
Set 5: 11Kcal in 25 seconds

Stop. Start again next week.

Once you can complete ten sets perfectly, then progress to the 30-second testing protocols. Remember, you are only to follow this for 6 weeks! Anything beyond 6 weeks and we tend to see a dramatic increase in fatigue and performance levels drop across the board. The final workout could look something like this:

WORKOUT RG - EXAMPLE

Warm-Up

Specific Activation Work:
Three rounds. No rest.

A1 Single Leg Kettlebell Deadlift x 5/5
A2 Overhead Kettlebell Squat x 5/5
A3 Dumbbell Side Plank Rotations x 5/5

Workout:
Part 1: Appetizer
Total Time: 15 Min.

15-Minute Circuit

A1 Single Leg Barbell RDL, 5/5 at 70% Max
A2 One Arm One Leg Row 5/5 at 70% Max
A3 Offset Barbell Lunges 5/5 + Bar + 10kg
A4 Single Arm Kettlebell Carry 30 sec
**   / 30 sec at 24kg**

Repeat. Continuous Work. No Rest.
This is the appetizer for the main event.

Part 2: Alactic Rowing Gainzzz

Row 13 calories in 25 seconds.
Rest 2:30 minutes.

Repeat until you can no longer hit 13 calories or have completed 10 rounds.

Tip: 25 Second Intervals: Set rower to 13 calories and 2:30 minutes rest intervals.

Stretch

The Lactate Bath

THE LACTATE BATH - LB

Warm-Up

Workout:
Set interval timer 05:00/00:30.
Run for 45 Min at MAF.

Every 5 Minutes perform 50% max push ups and then sprint as hard as possible for 30 seconds.

After each sprint, bring HR back down below MAF as fast as possible and then continue running at MAF.

Repeat.

Stretch

The Lactate Bath - Notes

Anaerobic Threshold Building

This workout has one primary purpose: **to teach the body to remove lactate faster** by using blood flow restriction and interval training techniques. As you perform push-ups, you will be restricting blood flow into the working muscles, then immediately see a surge of blood flow into them during the 30-second sprint phase.

Running at MAF and getting your heart rate back down is the key to this workout as we need to teach the body to recover faster. You may find that you initially need to walk a lot during the 4-minute recovery phase as your body hasn't yet discovered how to recover fast enough for the next interval.

Max Push-Up Testing

Prior to starting this workout, test your maximum amount of strict push-ups that you can do. This means at a pace of 3 seconds down, 1 second pause and then 1 second up. Your nose should almost be touching the floor on each push-up.

Progression

The progression of this workout is simple. It's all about reducing the time you need to get back to running at MAF. The 45-minute time limit stays the same.

The rules are the same throughout:

1. **Complete all 50% max push-ups**

2. **Sprint as hard as you can for 30 seconds.**

3. **Start running again immediately during the 4 minute recovery stage once your heart rate is back to below your MAF level, and keep it there.**

Alternatives to Running

Some days it may not be possible to run, or past injuries may not make this possible. Don't worry. We have alternative solutions. Simply choose from one of the three following pieces of equipment and switch running for one of these:

- **Assault Bike**
- **Concept 2 Rower**
- **Ski Erg**

Example: Lactate Bath Workout

WORKOUT LB - EXAMPLE

Warm-Up

Workout:

Set interval timer 05:00/00:30.

Run for 45 Min at 149 heart rate.

Every 5 Minutes perform 15 push ups and then sprint as hard as possible for 30 seconds.

After each sprint, bring HR back down below 149 as fast as possible and then continue running at 149.

Repeat.

Stretch

Workout - Walk/Run

Warm-Up

Workout:

Total time 60 minutes.

Option A - Walk/Run 60 Min (Run 2 min, Walk 3 min) at MAF

Option B - Run 60 Min at MAF (180 - Age)

At the end of 60 minutes, you should feel like you could keep going for another 2 hours. This is easy aerobic work.

Stretch

Walk/Run - Notes

Aerobic Base Building Continued:

The more aerobic we are, the more resilient we can be in life. We ask that you do not underestimate the importance of the Walk/Run prescription. This is all about developing the aerobic threshold you put in during Phase 1 so that we can help speed up recovery between higher-intensity workouts in Phase 3.

Option A or B: You Choose

We have provided two options for you here, which depend entirely on:

- **Your experience and ability to run**

- **How your body is feeling on this particular day**

If you are relatively new to running having completed phase 1, we recommend going with Option A in week 1, then potentially progressing to Option B in week 4 or 5. For the advanced and more experienced runner, Option 2 might be the best option. Either way, listen to your body and choose an option that best fits how you feel on that particular day.

For Option B Athletes Only:

If you decide to run the entire time at MAF, you will need to train in your MAF training zone. This means you have to keep your heart rate no lower than 10 beats per your score and never over.

Working Example:

Age = 40

MAF = 180 - 40 = 140

HR Training Range = 130 - 140 at all times.

The Progression

The progression of this is relatively straight forward. Over the weeks, we want to monitor the distance covered and the speed at which you perform this, all while keeping your heart rate below MAF. This is the key. It's about fundamentally developing your aerobic speed. Please **don't stray above your MAF heart rate**. This is key. It's a recovery run just as much as it is a recovery piece. If you feel tired on a given day, choose the easier option. It's not about going guns a blazing: it's about leaving you fresh for the next session.

The rules are similar to Phase 1 and 2:

- **You must feel refreshed and energized at the end of each workout.**

- **You never exceed your MAF heart rate.**

Hike

Warm-Up

Workout:

Total time: Minimum - 90 minutes.
Maximum - 4 Hours.

Get outside in the fresh air. Find a hill or mountain, the steeper the better, and build some good miles into your legs.

*For advanced athletes, wear a weight vest 10-40lbs.

Stretch

Hike - Notes

The benefits of hiking go far beyond working out, even though we are building miles into your legs here. A good walk outside or a regular hike can have a huge impact on our mental health, allowing us to switch off from stressful thoughts and think more rationally, all while being at one with nature.

We're big fans of hiking at Strength Matters as it:

1. **Will help clear your mind**

2. **Boost your brain and restore cognitive functions**

3. **Improve your outlook on life**

4. **Get you to unplug from the digital world**

Get outside, get some vitamin D, and enjoy nature. You'll be surprised how it will impact your training over the course of this training plan.

Hill Sprints - HS

Warm-Up

Workout:

Part 1:
Jog 1 Mile, Easy at MAF

Part 2:
Hill Sprints (Steeper the better)
Sprint Up The Hill as far as possible in 10 seconds.
Mark the distance.
Rest 2 Minutes.
Repeat. (Maximum 10 Sets)

*Do not add sets unless you reach the distance marked.

Part 3:
Jog 1 Mile, Easy at MAF

Stretch

Hill Sprint - Notes

You will be giving a 110% effort here. This is not for the faint hearted, but at the same time, you need to be controlled and measured in what you do. It's imperative you do this on a hill, the steeper the better for safety reasons, to reduce the element of injury to your hamstrings. Similar to the Rowing Gainzzz workout, there are certain rules you have to follow to get maximum benefits and ensure you stay fresh enough to complete all the other workouts during the week.

Testing Prior to This Workout

Prior to this workout, you will need to test the following:

Maximum distance sprinted in 10 seconds.

Set a 10-second countdown timer to buzz, or ask a friend to help you. Either way get a start and finish point. You can have three attempts with as much rest as you need in between. What you're looking for is your best distance.

For example:

Effort One = 20 meters

Effort Two = 22 meters

Effort Three = 24 meters

Your best score here would be 24 meters, and that is your goal for each 10 second interval.

The Hill Sprint Workout

I can't emphasize the importance of sticking to the rules in this workout. This is not about making yourself sick or trying to complete all ten sets every single week. This is about following the alactic development rules of engagement. The goal is to complete ten sets of X number of meters with a 2-minute rest perfectly. What I mean by perfectly is that all your sets are identical in nature. So that means, if your score was 24 meters in testing, ten sets of 24 meters with 2-minute rest in between.

If you produce results like this…

Set 1: 24 meters in 10 seconds

Set 2: 24 meters in 10 seconds

Set 3: 24 meters in 10 seconds

Set 4: 24 meters in 10 seconds

Set 5: 21 meters in 10 seconds

… you are done for the day.

We are flirting with your alactic anaerobic threshold, not trying to exceed it and completely fatigue the central nervous system. You must stop to give your body ample time to rest and recuperate for the other workouts. If you don't stick to this protocol, it will have a detrimental effect on your results.

On the flip side, if you produce perfect results the first time up of 10 perfect sets, I would suggest re-testing your max 10-second meter test. This is all about going to the point of failure. At seconds 11 and 12, you should be done and out for the count, not like you can go again immediately.

If it is still the same, continue the progression (outlined below), but then later drop back down to the 10-second protocol. This maybe the kick-starter your alactic anaerobic system needs to allow you to go deep enough into your central nervous system.

Hill Sprint Workout Progression

The progression of this workout is time and volume based. Once you can complete ten sets of 10-second intervals perfectly (all calories the same), you will re-start the process, except you increase the time to 12 seconds. This means re-testing your 12-second calorie marker and starting again. You will follow this process, adding 2 seconds up to a maximum of 20 seconds.

It goes:

1. **10 Second Intervals + 2 Min Rest**
2. **12 Second Intervals + 2:30 Min Rest**
3. **14 Second Intervals + 3 Min Rest**
4. **16 Second Intervals + 3:30 Min Rest**
5. **18 Second Intervals + 4 Min Rest**
6. **20 Second Intervals + 4:30 Min Rest**

It is highly unlikely you will reach 20 seconds in 6 weeks. If that is the case, the protocol hasn't been completed effectively and/or you are not strong enough to go deep into your alactic anaerobic system. If you can complete ten sets of 10-second intervals perfectly, followed by 12 seconds the next week and then 14 seconds the week after, you need to drop back down to 10 seconds and re-test to follow the protocol. In theory, this should not be possible, but we know it can happen when people don't have the capacity yet to dig deep into this part of the nervous system.

14 Second Working Example:

14 Second Test:

Effort One = 31 meters

Effort Two = 33 meters

Effort Three = 29 meters

Your best score here would be 33 meters, and that is your goal for each 14-second interval.

Example: first effort workout at 14 second intervals:

Set 1: 33 meters in 14 seconds

Set 2: 33 meters in 14 seconds

Set 3: 33 meters in 14 seconds

Set 4: 33 meters in 14 seconds

Set 5: 27 meters in 14 seconds

Stop. Start again next week.

Once you can complete ten sets perfectly, then progress to the 16-second testing protocols. Remember, you are only to follow this for 6 weeks! Anything after 6 weeks and we tend to see a dramatic increase in fatigue, and performance levels drop across the board.

HILL SPRINTS - HS EXAMPLE

Warm-Up

Workout:

Part 1:

Jog 1 Mile, Easy at 149 heart rate

Part 2:

Hill Sprints (Steeper the better)

Sprint 33 meters in 14 seconds.

Rest 3 Minutes.

Repeat. (Maximum 10 Sets)

*Do not add sets unless you reach the distance marked.

Part 3:

Jog 1 Mile, Easy at 149 heart rate

Stretch

Final Note & Disclaimer

Everybody likes to train differently.

This program is not designed for or tailored to anybody specifically. All weights and repetitions are a guide only, and you should only work within your capabilities.

The Strength Matters team strongly recommends that you consult with your physician before beginning any exercise program. You should be in good physical condition and be able to participate in most, if not all the exercises.

You should understand that when participating in any exercise or exercise program, there is the possibility of physical injury. If you engage in this exercise or exercise program, you agree that **you do so at your own risk**, are voluntarily participating in these activities, assume all risk of injury to yourself, and agree to release and discharge Strength Matters from any liability.

Now that's all said ... ENJOY!!

James Breese
Strength Matters Founder
Everyday Athlete

STRENGTH MATTERS®

MADE FOR **LIFE**

Fit Over Thirty

A podcast for people over thirty who want to lose weight, get stronger, and live better.

Stand on the shoulders of giants and learn from the greatest minds in health and fitness today! With killer interviews, inspiring stories and actionable strategies. Hosted by Josh Kennedy.

www.strengthmatters.com/podcasts

STRENGTH MATTERS®

MADE FOR **LIFE**

Bibliography

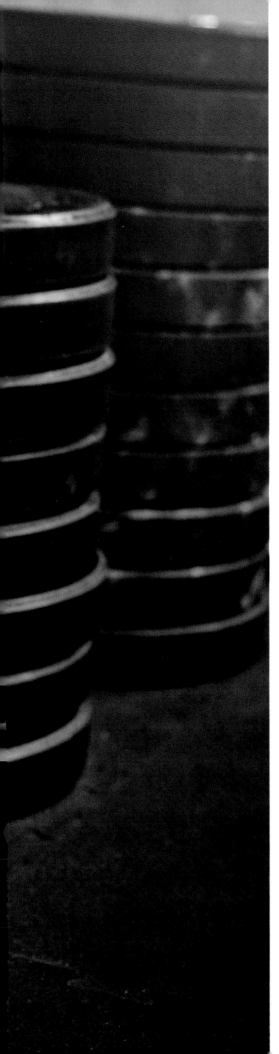

The Strength Matters Training Series is supported by thousands of hours of practical implementation, and research papers across the cognitive, physiologic, biochemical, biomechanical, and motor behavior sciences. It is far outside the scope of this book to provide an exhaustive list of all this research.

Instead, you will find here a list of books, authors, and training providers, that have greatly influenced the Strength Matters Training Series over the years.

- **8-Weeks Out,** Joel Jamieson
- **80/20 Running: Run Stronger and Race Faster By Training Slower,** Matt Fitzgerald
- **Advances in Functional Training,** Michael Boyle
- **Anatomy Trains,** Thomas Myers
- **Athletic Body in Balance,** Gray Cook
- **Atomic Habits,** James Clear
- **Intervention,** Dan John
- **Lore of Running,** Tim Noakes
- **Movement: Functional Movement Systems,** Gray Cook, Lee Burton, Kyle Kiesel, Greg Rose, and Milo Bryant
- **OPEX Fitness,** James Fitzgerald
- **Original Strength,** Tim Anderson
- **Periodization: Theory and Methodology of Training,** Tudor Bompa and Gregory Haff
- **Precision Nutrition,** Dr. John Berardi
- **Stop Chasing Pain,** Dr. Perry Nickelston
- **Supertraining,** Yuri V. Verkhoshanksy, Mel C. Siff
- **Run Strong,** Andrew Read
- **Taylor Starch**
- **The Big Book of Endurance Training and Racing,** Dr. Phil Maffetone
- **The Oxygen Advantage: The simple, scientifically proven breathing technique that will revolutionise your health and fitness,** Patrick McKeown
- **Training For The Uphill Athlete: A Manual For Mountain Runners and Ski Mountaineers,** Steve House and Scott Johnson
- **Ultimate Back Fitness and Performance,** Stuart McGill
- **Why We Sleep: The New Science of Sleep and Dreams,** Matthew Walker

Glossary

A

ACTIVATION WORK: Exercises and drills designed to prepare the nervous system for the work you are about to do. The principle behind this is to switch on the key muscles, that will be used during the workout, to help prevent injury and improve your performance.

AEROBIC: Relating to, involving, or requiring free oxygen, and refers to the use of oxygen to adequately meet energy demands during exercise via aerobic metabolism.

AEROBIC BASE: The physiological state in an athlete brought about by extensive training at low-to-moderate intensities. This type of training enhances the athlete's ability to produce energy aerobically and use fat as the primary fuel source. It supports higher-intensity anaerobic threshold work by allowing the athlete to recover faster and go deeper into the central nervous system to elicit the correct response.

AEROBIC CAPACITY: The highest amount of oxygen consumed during maximal exercise in activities that use the large muscle groups in the legs or arms and legs combined.

AEROBIC DEFICIENCY SYNDROME (ADS): A condition common in athletes who spend too much training time doing high-intensity efforts. This causes increased development of the anaerobic metabolic pathway and reduced development of the aerobic metabolic pathway. Ultimately, this will see a lowering of the Aerobic Threshold if continued for too long and decreased performance in endurance activities.

AEROBIC ENDURANCE: The ability of the cardiorespiratory system to work efficiently, supplying nutrients and oxygen to working muscles during sustained physical activity. At Strength Matters, we consider this to be continuous activities lasting over 60-minutes in duration.

AEROBIC POWER: The ability of the muscles to use oxygen received from the heart and lungs to produce energy. The more efficient this process becomes; the more aerobic power improves. Aerobic power is usually monitored and tested using VO2 max.

AEROBIC THRESHOLD: The aerobic threshold is the uppermost limit of exercise when the production of energy starts to become dominated by anaerobic glycolysis (sugars) rather than the oxidation (aerobic in nature) of fats.

AEROBIC TRAINING: Physical exercise of low intensity that depends primarily on the aerobic energy-generating process. Generally, light-to-moderate intensity activities that are sufficiently supported by aerobic metabolism that can be performed for extended periods.

AGILITY: The ability to move and change direction and position of the body quickly and effectively while under control. It is one of the ten components of complete athleticism and sits in Layer 3 of the Strength Matters Hierarchy of Athletic Development.

ANAEROBIC: Living, active, occurring or existing in the absence of free oxygen, as opposed to aerobic which means living, active, or occurring only in the presence of oxygen.

ANAEROBIC CAPACITY: Maximal work performed during maximum-intensity short-term physical effort; reflects the energy output capacity of the anaerobic metabolic pathway.

ANAEROBIC ENDURANCE: The ability to sustain intense, short-duration activity such as weightlifting or sprinting. Anaerobic endurance can be sub-divided as follows: Short anaerobic - less than 20 seconds (mainly alactic). Medium anaerobic - 20 seconds to 60 seconds (mainly lactic). Long anaerobic - 60 seconds to 120 seconds (lactic +aerobic).

ANAEROBIC THRESHOLD: The lowest intensity of exercise at which the production of lactate exceeds the muscle's ability to take up and utilize that lactate as fuel in aerobic metabolism. Above this intensity, lactate levels in the blood begin to rise. The greater the intensity above the anaerobic threshold, the greater the rise in blood lactate.

ANAEROBIC TRAINING: Is a physical exercise intense enough to cause lactate to form. It is used by athletes in non-endurance sports to promote strength, speed, and power, and by bodybuilders to build muscle mass. Muscle energy systems trained using anaerobic exercise develop differently compared to aerobic exercise, leading to greater performance in short duration, high-intensity activities, which last from mere seconds to up to about 2 minutes. Energy is drawn from a limited supply of stored muscle glycogen to support this short burst of intense activity.

ATHLETICISM: The physical qualities that are characteristic of athletes. At Strength Matters, we define athleticism as having ten components of complete athleticism; Mobility, stability, balance and coordination, strength, aerobic capacity, anaerobic capacity, speed, power, agility, and mental resilience.

BALANCE: The ability to stay upright or stay in control of body movement. There are two types of balance: static and dynamic. Static balance is maintaining equilibrium when stationary, while dynamic balance is maintaining equilibrium when moving.

CARDIO: From Classical Greek *kardia*, meaning heart. When you're doing cardio, it means you are exercising to improve the health of your heart.

CARDIOVASCULAR EXERCISE: Exercising at a constant level of easy intensity for a specified duration, a minimum of 30 minutes, and potentially lasting hours in duration. It is performed at an intensity at which the cardiovascular system can replenish oxygen to working muscles.

CARDIOVASCULAR FITNESS: A good measure of the heart's ability to pump oxygen-rich blood to the muscles.

CARDIOVASCULAR TRAINING: Cardiovascular training improves the ability of the heart, lungs, and blood vessels to deliver oxygen to the rest of the body.

CENTRAL NERVOUS SYSTEM (CNS): Controls most functions of the body and mind. It consists of two parts: the brain and the spinal cord. The brain is the center of our thoughts, the interpreter of our external environment, and the origin of control over body movement. The spinal cord is the highway of communication between the body and the brain.

COORDINATION: The ability to move two or more body parts under control, smoothly and efficiently. Coordination is a complex skill that also requires good balance, and good levels of other athletic components such strength and agility.

EVERYDAY ATHLETE: A person who prioritizes a healthy and physically active lifestyle in order to live life to the fullest.

EVERYDAY ATHLETE ETHOS:
I Love Life
I'm A Work In Progress
I Inspire Others
I Embrace Challenge
I am an Everyday Athlete

LACTATE THRESHOLD (see Anaerobic Threshold): The highest intensity at which lactate removal is matched by lactate production. Above this intensity lactate begins to accumulate rapidly. Any intensity above the Lactate Threshold will be unsustainable. The higher the intensity the less time it can be sustained.

MAXIMAL AEROBIC ENDURANCE: Defined by Strength Matters as the highest amount of oxygen consumed during maximal endurance activities with the ability to extend this type of exercise out to hours and hours of work.

MAXIMAL AEROBIC POWER: Maximal aerobic power is the highest peak oxygen uptake that an individual can obtain during dynamic exercise using large muscle groups during a few minutes performed under normal conditions at sea level.

MAXIMUM AEROBIC FUNCTION: A term first coined by Dr. Philip Maffetone to highlight the significance and importance of the aerobic energy system. Often abbreviated as MAF. Calculated using the formula 180 - your age

MENTAL RESILIENCE: Having the natural or developed psychological edge that enables you to: generally, cope better than your opponents with the many demands (competition, training, lifestyle) that sport places on a performer; specifically, be more consistent and better than your opponents in remaining determined, focused, confident, and in control under pressure.

METABOLIC ECONOMY: There are two metabolic pathways that create fuel for the body: aerobic metabolism and anaerobic glycolysis. Aerobic metabolism is the most efficient because it primarily uses fat as the major fuel source, which is a virtually unlimited supply of energy. Metabolic economy is the body choosing to use the most efficient fuel source for the task in hand.

MOBILITY: Flexibility in motion. The range of motion through muscles and joints.

POWER: The ability to create maximal force in minimal time.

SPEED: The ability to minimize the time cycle of a given movement.

STABILITY: The ability to prevent movement in one part of the body while creating movement in another, thus protecting vulnerable areas.

STRENGTH: Physical strength is the measure of an exertion of force on physical objects. Increasing physical strength is the goal of strength training.

TECHNICAL PROFICIENCY: The ability to perform a movement, in each sport, or exercise to the best your ability.

VO2 MAX: The maximum volume of oxygen you are capable of taking up and utilizing during intense exercise. It is measured in milliliters of oxygen used in a minute divided by the body weight in kilograms (ml/kg/min). It provides an aerobic power-to-weight ratio.

Index

About
Strength
Matters

It started in 2010 with an idea.

Strength Matters, previously known as Kettlebell Fever, started in 2010 as a kettlebell distribution company. In 2015, we morphed to match the growing needs and demands of our global community of everyday athletes over thirty. And we've been on an epic journey ever since.

From our beginnings as a fitness equipment manufacturer, we launched a print magazine and hosted events in London, San Diego, Chicago, Melbourne, and Munich. We've stayed true to our values - humility, excellence, respect - and to our commitment to deliver an exceptional experience across all our media platforms.

Today, Strength Matters is a complete media brand with print, audio, and online elements - not to mention our ever-expanding online personal coaching services. Based in Cardiff, Wales, we have an international reach and continue to grow and flourish. At our core is the simple belief that there is a better way for people over thirty to do health and fitness - a more intelligent, more sustainable approach that allows us to live life to the fullest well into our senior years.

We believe that there will always be a place for a print media brand committed to sharing the latest evidence, research, and trends in health and fitness, without selling out to the corporate marketing machine of the fitness industry.

And we know our success comes down to the readers, members, collaborators, and friends who support us along the way.

Meet the Author

Go where you feel most alive.

James Breese, Strength Matters Founder.

Besides chief dream maker at Strength Matters, James Breese is an author, speaker, podcaster, and vlogger. Born and raised on a farm in mid-wales, he's always had a passion for team sports and speaking foreign languages. Educated at Cardiff University, he studied French and German and completed a master's in computer science. Deciding against life in the corporate sector, he went in search of something more adventurous. He joined the Metropolitan Police Service, starting his career in Brixton, London.

Always the adventurer, it was during his time in the Met that he realized his true calling lay outside the police. He left the police in 2012 as his love for the mountains, snowboarding, and health and fitness became clear. Since forming Strength Matters in 2015, he's been on a mission to help everyday athletes over thirty lose weight, get stronger, and live better.

When he's not on an airplane or speaking on stage, you'll find James in the mountains of Wales or Austria, living the everyday athlete lifestyle. And when he's not in the mountains, you'll find him drinking coffee, going to the cinema, listening to live music, playing cricket, and watching his beloved Wales rugby and Manchester United soccer teams with friends.

You can connect with James on Instagram **@jamesbreese** or visit his website, **jamesbreese.com**.

Notes